CW00601605

How to access your on-line resources

Kaplan Financial students will have a MyKaplan account and these extra resources will be available to you online. You do not need to register again, as this process was completed when you enrolled. If you are having problems accessing online materials, please ask your course administrator.

If you are not studying with Kaplan and did not purchase your book via a Kaplan website, to unlock your extra online resources please go to www.en-gage.co.uk (even if you have set up an account and registered books previously). You will then need to enter the ISBN number (on the title page and back cover) and the unique pass key number contained in the scratch panel below to gain access.

You will also be required to enter additional information during this process to set up or confirm your account details.

If you purchased through Kaplan Flexible Learning or via the Kaplan Publishing website you will automatically receive an e-mail invitation to register your details and gain access to your content. If you do not receive the e-mail or book content, please contact Kaplan Publishing.

Your code and information

This code can only be used once for the registration of one book online. This registration and your online content will expire when the final sittings for the examinations covered by this book have taken place. Please allow one hour from the time you submit your book details for us to process your request.

Please scratch the film to access your unique code.

Please be aware that this code is case-sensitive and you will need to include the dashes within the passcode, but not when entering the ISBN.

Operational Level

Subject E1

Organisational Management

EXAM PRACTICE KIT

Published by: Kaplan Publishing UK

Unit 2 The Business Centre, Molly Millars Lane, Wokingham, Berkshire RG41 2QZ

Notice

British Library Cataloguing in Publication Data

A catalogue record for this book is available from the British Library

ISBN: 978-1-78415-932-0

Printed and bound in Great Britain

CONTENTS

	Page
Index to questions and answers	P.4
Examination techniques	P.5
Syllabus guidance, learning objectives and verbs	P.7
Approach to revision	P.11

Section

1	Objective test questions	1
2	Answers to objective test questions	53

Quality and accuracy are of the utmost importance to us so if you spot an error in any of our products, please send an email to mykaplanreporting@kaplan.com with full details.

Our Quality Co-ordinator will work with our technical team to verify the error and take action to ensure it is corrected in future editions.

INDEX TO QUESTIONS AND ANSWERS

OBJECTIVE TEST QUESTIONS

EXAM TECHNIQUES

COMPUTER-BASED ASSESSMENT

TEN GOLDEN RULES

1   Make sure you have completed the compulsory 15 minute tutorial before you start exam. This tutorial is available through the CIMA website. You cannot speak to the invigilator once you have started.

2   These exam practice kits give you plenty of exam style questions to practise so make sure you use them to fully prepare.

3   Attempt all questions, there is no negative marking.

4   Double check your answer before you put in the final answer although you can change your response as many times as you like.

5   On multiple choice questions (MCQs), there is only one correct answer.

6   Not all questions will be MCQs – you may have to fill in missing words or figures.

7   Identify the easy questions first and get some points on the board to build up your confidence.

8   Try and allow 15 minutes at the end to check your answers and make any corrections.

9   If you don't know the answer, flag the question and attempt it later. In your final review before the end of the exam try a process of elimination.

10 Work out your answer on the whiteboard provided first if it is easier for you. There is also an on-screen 'scratch pad' on which you can make notes. You are not allowed to take pens, pencils, rulers, pencil cases, phones, paper or notes.

SYLLABUS GUIDANCE, LEARNING OBJECTIVES AND VERBS

A AIMS OF THE SYLLABUS

The aims of the syllabus are

- to provide for the Institute, together with the practical experience requirements, an adequate basis for assuring society that those admitted to membership are competent to act as management accountants for entities, whether in manufacturing, commercial or service organisations, in the public or private sectors of the economy
- to enable the Institute to examine whether prospective members have an adequate knowledge, understanding and mastery of the stated body of knowledge and skills
- to complement the Institute's practical experience and skills development requirements.

B STUDY WEIGHTINGS

A percentage weighting is shown against each topic in the syllabus. This is intended as a guide to the proportion of study time each topic requires.

All component learning outcomes will be tested and one question may cover more than one component learning outcome.

The weightings do not specify the number of marks that will be allocated to topics in the examination.

C LEARNING OUTCOMES

Each topic within the syllabus contains a list of learning outcomes, which should be read in conjunction with the knowledge content for the syllabus. A learning outcome has two main purposes:

1 to define the skill or ability that a well-prepared candidate should be able to exhibit in the examination

2 to demonstrate the approach likely to be taken by examiners in examination questions.

The learning outcomes are part of a hierarchy of learning objectives. The verbs used at the beginning of each learning outcome relate to a specific learning objective, e.g. Evaluate alternative approaches to budgeting.

The verb 'evaluate' indicates a high-level learning objective. As learning objectives are hierarchical, it is expected that at this level students will have knowledge of different budgeting systems and methodologies and be able to apply them.

A list of the learning objectives and the verbs that appear in the syllabus learning outcomes and examinations follows and these will help you to understand the depth and breadth required for a topic and the skill level the topic relates to.

Learning objectives	Verbs used	Definition
1 Knowledge		
What you are expected to know	List	Make a list of
	State	Express, fully or clearly, the details of/ facts of
	Define	Give the exact meaning of
2 Comprehension		
What you are expected to understand	Describe	Communicate the key features of
	Distinguish	Highlight the differences between
	Explain	Make clear or intelligible/State the meaning of
	Identify	Recognise, establish or select after consideration
	Illustrate	Use an example to describe or explain something
3 Application		
How you are expected to apply your knowledge	Apply	To put to practical use
	Calculate/compute	To ascertain or reckon mathematically
	Demonstrate	To prove with certainty or to exhibit by practical means
	Prepare	To make or get ready for use
	Reconcile	To make or prove consistent/ compatible
	Solve	Find an answer to
	Tabulate	Arrange in a table
4 Analysis		
How you are expected to analyse the detail of what you have learned	Analyse	Examine in detail the structure of
	Categorise	Place into a defined class or division
	Compare and contrast	Show the similarities and/or differences between
	Construct	To build up or compile
	Discuss	To examine in detail by argument
	Interpret	To translate into intelligible or familiar terms
	Produce	To create or bring into existence
5 Evaluation		
How you are expected to use your learning to evaluate, make decisions or recommendations	Advise	To counsel, inform or notify
	Evaluate	To appraise or assess the value of
	Recommend	To advise on a course of action
	Advise	To counsel, inform or notify

D OBJECTIVE TEST

The most common types of Objective Test questions are:

- multiple choice, where you have to choose the correct answer(s) from a list of possible answers. This could either be numbers or text.

- multiple choice with more choices and answers — for example, choosing two correct answers from a list of eight possible answers. This could either be numbers or text.

- single numeric entry, where you give your numeric answer e.g. profit is $10,000.

- multiple entry, where you give several numeric answers e.g. the charge for electricity is $2000 and the accrual is $200.

- true/false questions, where you state whether a statement is true or false e.g. external auditors report to the directors is FALSE.

- matching pairs of text e.g. the convention 'prudence' would be matched with the statement' inventories revalued at the lower of cost and net realisable value'.

- other types could be matching text with graphs and labelling graphs/diagrams.

In this Exam Practice Kit we have used these types of questions.

Some further guidance from CIMA on number entry questions is as follows:

- For number entry questions, you do not need to include currency symbols or other characters or symbols such as the percentage sign, as these will have been completed for you. You may use the decimal point but must not use any other characters when entering an answer (except numbers) so, for example, $10,500.80 would be input as 10500.80

- When expressing a decimal, for example a probability or correlation coefficient, you should include the leading zero (i.e. you should input 0.5 not .5)

- Negative numbers should be input using the minus sign, for example −1000

- You will receive an error message if you try to enter a character or symbol that is not permitted (for example a '£' or '%' sign)

- A small range of answers will normally be accepted, taking into account sensible rounding

Guidance re CIMA On-Screen calculator:

As part of the computer based assessment software, candidates are now provided with a calculator. This calculator is on-screen and is available for the duration of the assessment. The calculator is accessed by clicking the calculator button in the top left hand corner of the screen at any time during the assessment.

All candidates must complete a 15 minute tutorial before the assessment begins and will have the opportunity to familiarise themselves with the calculator and practise using it.

Candidates may practise using the calculator by downloading and installing the practice exam at http://www.vue.com/athena/. The calculator can be accessed from the fourth sample question (of 12).

Please note that the practice exam and tutorial provided by Pearson VUE at http://www.vue.com/athena/ is not specific to CIMA and includes the full range of question types the Pearson VUE software supports, some of which CIMA does not currently use.

The Objective Tests are ninety minute computer-based assessments comprising 60 compulsory questions, with one or more parts. CIMA is continuously developing the question styles within the system and you are advised to try the online website demo at www.cimaglobal.com, to both gain familiarity with assessment software and examine the latest style of questions being used.

APPROACH TO REVISION

Stage 1: Assess areas of strengths and weaknesses

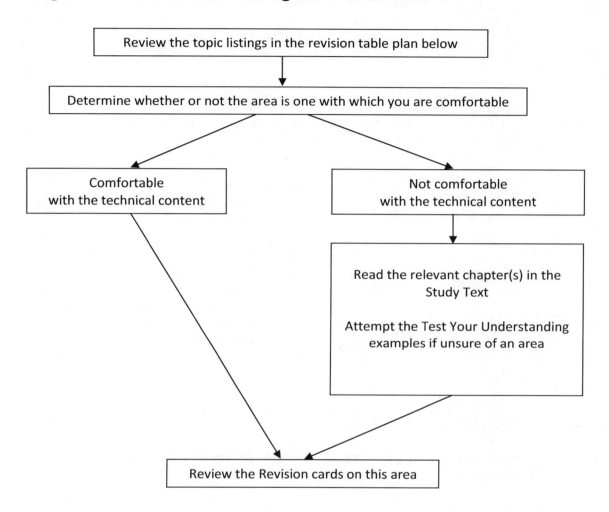

Review the topic listings in the revision table plan below

Determine whether or not the area is one with which you are comfortable

Comfortable
with the technical content

Not comfortable
with the technical content

Read the relevant chapter(s) in the
Study Text

Attempt the Test Your Understanding
examples if unsure of an area

Review the Revision cards on this area

Stage 2: Question practice

Follow the order of revision of topics as recommended in the revision table plan below and attempt the questions in the order suggested.

Try to avoid referring to text books and notes and the model answer until you have completed your attempt.

Try to answer the question in the allotted time.

Review your attempt with the model answer and assess how much of the answer you achieved in the allocated exam time.

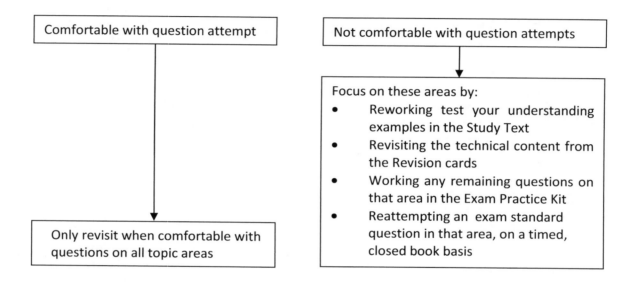

Stage 3: Final pre-exam revision

We recommend that you **attempt at least one ninety minute mock examination** containing a set of previously unseen exam standard questions.

It is important that you get a feel for the breadth of coverage of a real exam without advanced knowledge of the topic areas covered – just as you will expect to see on the real exam day.

Ideally a mock examination offered by your tuition provider should be sat in timed, closed book, real exam conditions.

E1
ORGANISATIONAL MANAGEMENT

Syllabus overview

E1 focuses on the structuring of organisations. It covers the structure and principles underpinning the operational functions of the organisation, their efficient management and effective interaction in enabling the organisation to achieve its strategic objectives. It lays the foundation for gaining further insight into both the immediate operating environment and long-term strategic future of organisations, which are covered in E2 and E3.

Summary of syllabus

Weight	Syllabus topic
25%	A. Introduction to organisations
15%	B. Managing the finance function
15%	C. Managing technology and information
15%	D. Operations management
15%	E. Marketing
15%	F. Managing human resources

E1 – A. INTRODUCTION TO ORGANISATIONS (25%)

Learning outcomes

On completion of their studies, students should be able to:

Lead	Component	Indicative syllabus content
1 discuss the different types of structure that an organisation may adopt.	(a) discuss the different purposes of organisations	• Ownership: – private sector, public sector. • Motive: – for-profit, non-profit. • Mission and vision: – shared values and beliefs. • Creating value for stakeholders: – control and coordination of resources to achieve goals and outcomes – efficient production of goods and services – facilitating innovation.
	(b) explain the different structures organisations may adopt	• Organisational configuration (Mintzberg): – technical core – technical support – administrative support – top and middle management. • Organisational configuration, contextual dimensions, the effect of: – technology – environment – culture. • Structural dimensions, influence of: – size – formalisation – specialisation – organisation type e.g. sole-trader, partnership, company, multinational. • Structural organisation: – functional – divisional – matrix – geographical.

Learning outcomes

On completion of their studies, students should be able to:

Lead	Component	Indicative syllabus content
	(c) explain the various forms and functional boundaries of the organisation including externalisation, shared service centres (SSC) and business process outsourcing (BPO).	• Closed and open systems. • Vertical and horizontal structures. • Outsourcing. • Alliances. • Virtual network structure.
2 discuss relationships between internal and external sources of governance, regulation and professional behaviour.	(a) discuss the purpose and principles of good corporate governance, the ethical responsibilities of the organisation and individuals, and ways of achieving corporate social responsibility.	• Corporate governance, including expectations of stakeholders and the role of government. • Creating an ethical organisation. • Principles of corporate social responsibility (CSR). • Developing business-government relations. • The impact of regulation on the organisation. • Role of institutions and governance in economic growth. • Personal business ethics and the fundamental principles (Part A) of the CIMA Code of Ethics for Professional Accountants.

E1 – B. MANAGING THE FINANCE FUNCTION (15%)

Learning outcomes
On completion of their studies, students should be able to:

Lead	Component	Indicative syllabus content
1 discuss the purpose of the finance function and its relationships with other parts of the organisation.	(a) demonstrate the contribution the finance function makes to the sustainable delivery of the organisation's strategies in a range of contexts	• Stewardship and control of physical and financial resources within the organisation. • Interpreting and reporting the financial position of the organisation for external stakeholders (including statutory requirements) and internal management. • Collating and providing information to enable efficient asset management and cost effective operation of the organisation. • Comparing the current position with forecast/budget expectations and indicating where and how differences have occurred. Providing this in a timely and accurate manner. • Assisting and interacting with other functions in providing solutions to variances.
	(b) analyse the components of the finance function (financial and management accounting, treasury, company secretarial and internal audit)	• Financial accounting – ensuring accurate asset values, efficient working capital management, statutory reporting. • Management accounting – operational reporting (profit and loss) cost control, variance analysis. • Treasury management – sourcing finance, currency management, effective taxation administration. • Company secretarial. • Internal audit – ensuring compliance, fraud detection and avoidance.
	(c) discuss the potential for conflict within the role of the finance function.	• Potential conflicts: – interdependence/independence. – short-term/long-term. – capital/revenue.

Learning outcomes

On completion of their studies, students should be able to:

Lead	Component	Indicative syllabus content
2 explain how the finance function supports the organisation's strategies and operations.	(a) explain the activities fundamental to the role of the finance function (accounting operations, analysis, planning, decision making and control)	• Preparation of statutory reports. • Preparation of plans, forecasts, budgets. • Working capital reporting and control, inventories, receivables, payables, cash. • Provision of analysis to support decisions. • Performance reporting, budget/actuals. • Cost reporting, product/process. • Ensuring systems in place to provide timely and accurate control information.
	(b) explain the contemporary transformation of the finance function.	• Reconfiguration: – bureaucratic to market oriented. • Shared services: – outsourced market orientation. • Business Process Re-engineering: – roles of process working. • Relocation: – retained/near-shore/off-shore. • Segregation of the finance function: – transactional/transformational activities. • Business partners: – support involvement.

E1 – C. MANAGING TECHNOLOGY AND INFORMATION (15%)

Learning outcomes
On completion of their studies, students should be able to:

Lead	Component	Indicative syllabus content
1 demonstrate the purpose of the technology and information function and its relationships with other parts of the organisation.	(a) demonstrate the value of information systems in organisations	• The role of information systems in organisations. • Emerging information system trends in organisations. The networked enterprise, organisational benefits, customer relationship management systems.
	(b) demonstrate ways of organising and managing information systems in the context of the wider organisation.	• Information technology – enabling transformation; the emergence of new, more virtual forms of organisation, technology infrastructure. • Geographically dispersed (virtual) teams; role of information systems in virtual teams and challenges for virtual collaboration. • Managing knowledge, enhancing internal and external relationships. • Ethical and social issues associated with information systems.
2 explain how information systems support the organisation's strategies and operations.	(a) explain the technical components and options for information technology system design	• Evaluating costs and benefits of information systems. • The internet, intranet, wireless technology, cloud technologies. • Privacy and security. • Overview of systems architecture and data flows. • Big Data information management: – large volumes of data – complexity and variety of data – velocity, real time data.
	(b) explain the role of emerging technologies e.g. Big Data, digitisation and their uses.	• Enhancing decision making support using Big Data and analytics: – identifying business value – relating to customer requirements – developing organisational blueprint – building capabilities on business priorities – ensuring measurable outcomes.

Learning outcomes

On completion of their studies, students should be able to:

Lead	Component	Indicative syllabus content
		• Information system implementation as a change management process; avoiding problems of non-usage and resistance.
		• System changeover methods (i.e. direct, parallel, pilot and phased).
		• Information system outsourcing (different types of sourcing strategies; client-vendor relationships).
		• E-commerce, digital markets, social media, digital goods.
		• Remote working, hot desking.
		• Big Data and digitisation: – addressing customer needs – effective and speedy decisions.

E1 – D. OPERATIONS MANAGEMENT (15%)

Learning outcomes
On completion of their studies, students should be able to:

Lead	Component	Indicative syllabus content
1 demonstrate the purpose of the operations function and its relationships with other parts of the organisation.	(a) demonstrate the contribution of operations management to the efficient production and delivery of fit-for-purpose goods and services	• Overview of operations strategy and its importance to the firm.
	(b) demonstrate how supply chains can be established and managed.	• Procurement as a strategic process in supply chain management. • Development of relationships with suppliers, including the use of supply portfolios. • Supply chains in competition with each other; role of supply networks; demand networks as an evolution of supply chains. • Design of products/services and processes and how this relates to operations and supply. • The concept of CSR and sustainability in operations management.
2 apply tools and techniques of operations management.	(a) apply the tools and concepts of operations management to deliver sustainable performance	• Process design. • Product and service design. • Supply network design. • Forecasting. • Layout and flow. • Process technology: – CNC, Robots, AGV, FMS, CIM – decision support systems – expert systems. • Work study. • Capacity planning and control, inventory control.

Learning outcomes

On completion of their studies, students should be able to:

Lead	Component	Indicative syllabus content

	(b) explain how relationships within the supply chain can be managed.	• Supply chain planning and control:
		  – lean synchronisation
		  – contractual/relational approaches
		  – material requirement planning
		  – quality planning and control
		  – statistical process control
		  – operational improvement, total quality management (TQM), Kaizen, Six Sigma, Lean thinking
		  – reverse logistics.

E1 – E. MARKETING (15%)

Learning outcomes
On completion of their studies, students should be able to:

Lead	Component	Indicative syllabus content
1 demonstrate the purpose of the marketing function and its relationships with other parts of the organisation.	(a) apply the marketing concept and principles in a range of organisational contexts	• The marketing concept as a business philosophy. • The marketing environment, including societal, economic, technological, political and legal factors affecting marketing (PESTEL). • The role of marketing in the business plan of the organisation. • Marketing in public sector and not-for-profit organisations e.g. charities, non-governmental organisations, etc.

	(b) apply the elements of the marketing mix.	• The 7 Ps:
		  – product
		  – place
		  – price
		  – promotion
		  – processes
		  – people
		  – physical evidence.
		• Theories of consumer behaviour (e.g. social interaction theory), as well as factors affecting buying decisions, types of buying behaviour and stages in the buying process.
		• Social marketing and CSR.
		• Social media and its effect on the organisation.

Learning outcomes

On completion of their studies, students should be able to:

Lead	Component	Indicative syllabus content

2 apply tools and techniques to formulate the organisation's marketing strategies, including the collection, analysis and application of Big Data.	(a) apply the main techniques of marketing	• Market research, including data gathering techniques and methods of analysis.
		• Segmentation and targeting of markets, and positioning of products within markets.
		• How business to business (B2B) and business to government (B2G) marketing differs from business to consumer (B2C) marketing in its different forms:
		  – consumer marketing
		  – services marketing
		  – direct marketing
		  – interactive marketing
		  – E-marketing
		  – internal marketing.
		• Promotional tools and the promotion mix.
		• The 'service extension' to the marketing mix.
		• Devising and implementing a pricing strategy.
		• Internal marketing as the process of training and motivating employees to support the firm's external marketing activities.
		• Relationship marketing.
		• Not-for-profit marketing.
		• Experiential marketing.
		• Postmodern marketing.

Learning outcomes

On completion of their studies, students should be able to:

Lead	Component	Indicative syllabus content
	(b) explain the role of emerging technologies and media in marketing.	<ul><li>Big Data analytics and its use in the marketing process:<ul><li>– predicting customer demand</li><li>– improving the customer experience</li><li>– monitoring multi-channel transactions</li><li>– identifying customer preferences.</li></ul></li><li>Marketing communications, including viral, guerrilla and other indirect forms of marketing.</li><li>Distribution channels and methods for marketing campaigns, including digital marketing.</li><li>Brand image and brand value.</li><li>Product development and product/service life-cycles.</li><li>The differences and similarities in the marketing of products, services and experiences.</li><li>Product portfolios and the product mix.</li><li>Marketing sustainability and ethics.</li></ul>

E1 – F. MANAGING HUMAN RESOURCES (15%)

Learning outcomes
On completion of their studies, students should be able to:

Lead	Component	Indicative syllabus content
1 **demonstrate the purpose of the HR function and its relationships with other parts of the organisation.**	(a) explain the contribution of HR to the sustainable delivery of the organisation's strategies	• The concept of HRM and its influence on organisational processes and performance. • The psychological contract and its importance to retention. • The relationship of the employee to other elements of the business. • HR in different organisational forms, project based, virtual or networked firms and different organisational contexts.

	(b) apply the elements of the HR cycle.	• Acquisition:
		  – identify staffing requirement
		  – recruitment
		  – selection.
		• Development:
		  – training
		  – evaluation
		  – progression.
		• Maintenance:
		  – monetary and non-monetary benefits.
		• Separation:
		  – voluntary and involuntary.

2 **apply the tools and techniques of HRM.**	(a) demonstrate the HR activities associated with developing employees	• Practices associated with recruiting and developing appropriate abilities including recruitment and selection of staff using different recruitment channels:
		  – interviews
		  – assessment centres, intelligence tests, aptitude tests
		  – psychometric tests
		  – competency frameworks.

Learning outcomes

On completion of their studies, students should be able to:

Lead	Component	Indicative syllabus content
		• Issues relating to fair and legal employment practices (e.g. recruitment, dismissal, redundancy, and ways of managing these).
		• The distinction between training and development, and the tools available to develop and train staff.
		• The design and implementation of induction programmes.
		• Practices related to motivation including issues in the design of reward systems: − the role of incentives − the utility of performance-related pay − arrangements for knowledge workers − flexible work arrangements.
	(b) demonstrate the role of the line manager in the implementation of HR practices.	• The importance of appraisals, their conduct and their relationship to the reward system.
		• Practices related to the creation of opportunities for employees to contribute to the organisation including: job design, communications, involvement procedures and principles of negotiation.
		• Problems in implementing HR plans appropriate to a team and ways to manage this.
		• Preparation of an HR plan. Forecasting personnel requirements: retention, absence and leave, employee turnover.
		• Ethical code and the interface with HR practice.

FORMULAE AND TABLES

Information concerning formulae and tables will be provided via the CIMA website, www.cimaglobal.com, and your EN-gage login.

Section 1

OBJECTIVE TEST QUESTIONS

All the section objective questions carry the same number of marks.

SYLLABUS SECTION A: INTRODUCTION TO ORGANISATIONS

1   Which of the following is NOT a key feature of an organisation?

   A   Controlled performance

   B   Collective goals

   C   Social arrangements

   D   Creation of a product or service

2   Which of the following organisations is normally found in the public sector?

   A   Schools

   B   Charities

   C   Clubs

   D   Businesses

3   The public sector is normally concerned with:

   A   making profit from the sale of goods

   B   providing services to specific groups funded from charitable donations

   C   the provision of basic government services

   D   raising funds by subscriptions from members to provide common services

4   A Co is a company which specialises in forestry. It has recently purchased B Co, which runs a chain of recreational resorts. A has allowed B to build several new resorts on land which is owned by A, but which it is no longer able to use. The resorts have proven highly profitable and popular. Which of the following best explains the reason for the improved performance of the combined entity?

   A   Specialisation

   B   Social interactivity

   C   Synergy

   D   Service

5 **Which of the following statements regarding limited companies is correct?**

A Public limited companies have access to a wider pool of finance than partnerships or sole traders.

B Both public and private limited companies are allowed to sell shares to the public.

C Companies are always owned by many different investors.

D Shareholders are liable for any debts the company may incur.

6 **Which of the following is a characteristic of ALL limited companies?**

A It has a separate legal personality

B It must employ fewer than 20 people

C The directors must hold at least 50% of the shares

D The public must own the vast majority of the shares, the remaining shares being owned by the directors

7 **Which of the following organisations would normally be classified as BOTH a not-for-profit organisation AND a private sector organisation? Select ALL that apply.**

A Government departments

B Partnerships

C Charities

D Companies

8 'An organisation that is owned and democratically controlled by its members.'

To which type of organisation does this definition relate?

A Charities

B Non-governmental organisations

C Co-operatives

D Private limited companies

9 **Which ONE of the following statements is true?**

A Partnerships offer the same benefits to investors as limited companies.

B Sole traders have no personal liability for business debts.

C Limited companies are classed as a separate legal entity; therefore the shareholders are not personally liable for any debts of the business.

D A partnership can be made up of no more than 20 partners.

10   Which TWO of the following characteristics are NOT normally associated with a Non-Governmental Organisation (NGO)?

    A   Furthering humanitarian causes

    B   Championing social causes

    C   Making profits

    D   Exercising independence

    E   Government funded

    F   Independent

    G   Non-profit making

    H   Explicit social mission

11   Non-political, not-for-profit, cause-orientated organisations drawn from more than one country are known as:

    A   strategic business units

    B   non-governmental organisations (NGOs)

    C   conglomerates

    D   globalised networks

12   Which of the following statements regarding the entrepreneurial structure is correct?

    A   It usually allows for defined career paths for employees

    B   It often enjoys strong goal congruence throughout the organisation

    C   It can normally cope with significant diversification and growth

    D   Control within the organisation tends to be weak

13   Which of the following is a disadvantage of a functional structure?

    A   Lack of economies of scale

    B   Absence of standardisation

    C   Specialists feel isolated

    D   Empire building

14   Which of the following structures is best placed to address the need for co-ordination between different functions in very complex situations?

    A   Functional

    B   Divisional

    C   Matrix

    D   Geographical

15 Which of the following is a characteristic of a matrix structure?

    A   Built around the owner manager, who makes all the decisions.

    B   Appropriate for small companies which have few products and locations and which exist in a relatively stable environment.

    C   Structured in accordance with product lines or divisions or departments.

    D   Requires dual reporting to managers, for example when a project team member has to report to a project manager as well as a head of his functional department.

16 The following are attributes of either divisional OR functional structures. Which TWO of the following are features of the DIVISIONAL structure?

    A   Economies of scale are encouraged

    B   Encourages standardisation of outputs and processes

    C   Adaptable if further diversification is pursued

    D   Senior managers are able to focus on strategic issues

17 H Co makes a variety of unrelated products, including bicycles, furniture and electronics. It is aware that each of these products requires very different strategies and functions. H wishes to use a structure that will allow for each product to be managed separately, but wishes to minimise its overall administrative costs.

Which of the following organisational structures would be most appropriate for H Co to adopt?

    A   Divisional

    B   Entrepreneurial

    C   Functional

    D   Matrix

18 Which of the following structures results in a potential loss of control over key operating decisions and a reduction in goal congruence?

    A   Matrix

    B   Entrepreneurial

    C   Functional

    D   Geographic

19 In relation to organisational structures which of the following is the correct definition of the phrase 'span of control'?

    A   The number of employees that a manager is directly responsible for

    B   The number of management levels in an organisational structure

    C   The number of levels in the hierarchy below a given manager

    D   The number of managers in the organisation

20 **Which ONE of the following factors would tend to allow an organisation to develop a wide span of control?**

A   Highly skilled, motivated employees

B   Employees spread over a wide geographical area

C   Employees undertake complex, changing tasks

D   Employees have low levels of motivation

21 G Co manufactures a product which is made of four components which are then bolted together. G is considering outsourcing the production of two of these components to an external company, though G would still assemble the final product itself.

Which ONE of the following boundaryless structures will G most closely match if it proceeds with this arrangement?

A   Hollow

B   Virtual

C   Modular

D   Entrepreneurial

22 **Transaction costs are expenses resulting from which ONE of the following?**

A   Outsourcing of services

B   Off-shoring of organisational functions

C   Penetration pricing

D   Organisational downsizing

23 **Transaction costs are associated with which ONE of the following?**

A   Materials procurement

B   Flexible working arrangements

C   Outsourcing

D   Lobbying

24 **Match the terms in the list below to the relevant description:**

- Vision

- Mission

Term	*Definition*
Mission	The most generalised type of objective. It can be seen as an expression of the organisation's reason for being.
Vision	Sets out how the organisation sees itself in the future.

25   A lack of physical presence and extensive use of IT are typical features of which sort of organisation?

A   Non-governmental organisations (NGO)

B   Multinational enterprises (MNE)

C   Shamrock organisations

D   Virtual organisations

26   Organisations that move part of their activities to another country are said to do which ONE of the following?

A   Downsize

B   Divest

C   Offshore

D   Outsource

27   Organisational costs associated with contracted out activities are known as which ONE of the following?

A   Transaction costs

B   Offshoring costs

C   Transfer costs

D   Social costs

28   Service Level Agreements are normally associated with which ONE of the following?

A   Job reductions negotiated with staff groups

B   Deskilling

C   Agreed appraisal outcomes

D   Outsourcing

29   Transferring some part of an organisation's activities to a subsidiary in another country is an example of:

A   free trade

B   outsourcing

C   offshoring

D   delegation

30   Expenses incurred through outsourcing are known as:

A   externalities

B   uncertainty costs

C   transaction costs

D   internal failure costs

31   **Which of the following statements relating to organisational structure are correct? Select ALL that apply.**

A   A virtual organisation exists where all non-core activities are outsourced to third parties.

B   A scalar chain refers to the number of levels of management within the organisation.

C   Entrepreneurial structures typically suffer from slow decision making.

D   An organisation's span of control is unaffected by the nature of the work the organisation undertakes.

E   Decentralisation tends to reduce training costs within the organisation.

F   A matrix structure may increase conflict between managers.

G   Tall organisations typically have a narrow span of control.

H   A 'shared services approach' refers to the centralisation of a previously dispersed function within the organisation.

32   **Where there are a large number of external shareholders who play no role in the day-to-day running of a company, there is a situation that is described as:**

A   detached corporate ownership

B   uninvolved external ownership

C   dividend based shareholding

D   separation of ownership and control

33   **Mendelow's four cell matrix illustrates which ONE of the following?**

A   The dominance of various stakeholders in a decision

B   The potential growth and market share of a product

C   The support required by a technostructure

D   The direction of organisational growth strategies

34   JM Co is a medium-sized clothing retail chain that has recently undertaken a stakeholder analysis exercise using Mendelow's matrix. JM feels that the national government currently has little interest in the company, though the directors feel that it would have significant power should it choose to intervene in the company's affairs.

What strategy would Mendelow's matrix suggest JM takes with regards to the national government?

A   Key players

B   Minimal effort

C   Keep satisfied

D   Keep informed

35 **The basis of the stakeholder view is that:**

    A   only shareholders are legitimate stakeholders

    B   only creditors and shareholders are legitimate stakeholders

    C   persons, groups and organisations with an interest in the organisation are stakeholders

    D   only members that an organisation officially recognises are stakeholders

36 **Gareth has recently been asked to join the board of HH plc as a non-executive director. Which of the following would mean that he is not sufficiently independent and should not accept the role? Select ALL that apply.**

    A   He retired from a managerial role in HH plc 7 years ago

    B   He holds a very small number of shares in HH plc

    C   He is a member of HH plc's corporate pension scheme

    D   He holds cross directorship

37 **Which of the following statements is correct regarding non-executive directors?**

    A   They should make up at least half of the board of directors in larger companies.

    B   They help the executive directors with the daily running of the company.

    C   They may be friends or relatives of the executive directors, as this helps their working relationship.

    D   Once appointed, they should continue to act as non-executives for as long as possible as this will ensure they are knowledgeable and experienced.

38 **Which ONE of the following is an independent member of a company's Board with particular concern for governance?**

    A   Non-executive director

    B   Management consultant

    C   Political lobbyist

    D   External examiner

39 **Lobbying by a business is an example of which ONE of the following?**

    A   Focus group research

    B   Country and political risk analysis

    C   Corporate social responsibility

    D   Political activity

40 The system of policies by which an organisation is directed and controlled is known as which ONE of the following?

    A   Corporate governance

    B   Corporate social responsibility

    C   Corporate infrastructure

    D   Corporate strategic apex

41 Corporate political activity often involves which ONE of the following?

    A   Clarifying corporate social responsibility

    B   Scanning the microenvironment

    C   Lobbying and political campaign contributions

    D   Internal marketing

42 Corporate governance is best described as:

    A   a code for organisational direction, administration and control

    B   stakeholder guidelines

    C   a system of penalties for unethical behaviour

    D   the relationship between an organisation and the government

43 Which ONE of the following is NOT a benefit of corporate governance?

    A   Improved access to capital markets

    B   Stimulation of performance

    C   Enhanced marketability of goods and services

    D   Prevention of fraudulent claims by contractors

44 Corporate political activity is normally undertaken in order to

    A   secure policy preferences

    B   make the world a better place

    C   further an environmental agenda

    D   understand the external drivers on an organisation

45 Which of the following is the best example of a closed system?

    A   Professional bureaucracy

    B   Simple structure

    C   Machine bureaucracy

    D   Divisionalised form

46 Efficient regulation of companies is said to exist if:

A the total benefit to the nation is greater than the total cost

B there is greater integration of the world's economies

C greater innovation takes place by all businesses

D the effect on businesses is neutral

47 The influence an organisation will normally have over its macro environment will be:

A limited or non-existent

B high

C extremely high

D continual

48 The 'agency problem' refers to which of the following situations?

A Shareholders acting in their own short-term interests rather than the long-term interests of the company.

B A vocal minority of shareholders expecting the directors to act as their agents and pay substantial dividends.

C Companies reliant upon substantial government contracts such that they are effectively agents of the government.

D The directors acting in their own interests rather than the shareholders' interests.

49 Which of the following would best explain the concept of sustainable development?

A Starting business in the developed countries where the economic climate is conducive to trade.

B Development which meets the needs of the present without compromising the ability of future generations to meet their own needs.

C Sustaining the production at the level of maximum capacity.

D Developing the business by signing long-term contracts with suppliers.

50 Intervention by government to impose a limit on businesses' carbon emissions is an example of regulation motivated by the wish to address market failure caused by:

A asymmetric information

B equity

C market imperfection

D externalities

51   The US Sarbanes-Oxley Act 2002 has no direct effect on companies incorporated and listed in the UK unless:

  A   they are part of a company regulated by the Securities and Exchange Commission

  B   they are part of a company listed on a US stock exchange

  C   they are part of a company with headquarters in the US

  D   they are part of a company with significant operations in the US

52   Which of the following would raise ethical issues for a manufacturer of chocolate? Select ALL that apply.

  A   The materials used in the production of the chocolate

  B   The quality of the chocolate

  C   How the chocolate is advertised

  D   How much its cocoa supplier pays its staff

  E   How much it pays its own staff

53   HGF Co is considering implementing a corporate social responsibility (CSR) policy. However it is concerned that there may be drawbacks to this. Which TWO of the following are possible problems caused by a CSR policy?

  A   Increased materials cost

  B   Failure to attract and retain quality employees

  C   Loss of management time

  D   Loss of key business skills

54   A Co is considering improving its impact on the environment by adopting a sustainable approach to business. Which of the following statements are correct with regards to A's decision (select ALL that apply)?

  A   It may help to reduce the organisation's operating costs

  B   It could lead to an improved relationship with shareholders and other stakeholders

  C   It may improve employee motivation

  D   It would be expected to reduce the administrative burden on management

55   Which THREE of the following are potential advantages of a shared service approach?

  A   Improved consistency of service

  B   Fewer resources will be required to migrate diverse systems

  C   Is always favourable to outsourcing to a third party

  D   Systems consolidation

  E   Cost savings through greater efficiency and reduced duplication of roles.

56 Choke Co purchases a number of raw materials from various suppliers and uses them to create material G. This material takes a long time to degrade in the environment and poses a risk to animal and plant life for several decades. Any stocks of G that have been unsold for more than one month are no longer saleable and have to be disposed of.

Which ONE of the following would be most helpful to Choke in minimising the impact that wastage of material G has on the environment?

A   Sourcing raw materials from environmentally friendly suppliers

B   Improved communication with customers to identify likely demand

C   Improved energy efficiency of the production process for material G

D   Reduction in packaging on the units of material G that are sold

57 **Mintzberg's design of an effective organisation does NOT include which ONE of the following categories?**

A   Technostructure

B   Outsource partners

C   Operating core

D   Strategic apex

58 **Match the principles from CIMA's Code of Ethics in the list below to the relevant interpretation:**

- Confidentiality
- Integrity
- Professional behaviour
- Professional competence and due care
- Objectivity

Principle	*Interpretation*
Competence	Maintaining a relevant level of professional knowledge and skills so that a competent service can be provided.
behaviour	Complying with relevant laws and regulations.
Integrity	Being straightforward, honest and truthful in all professional and business relationships.
Confid	Not disclosing information unless there is specific permission or a legal or professional duty to do so.
object	Not allowing bias, conflict of interest or the influence of other people to override professional judgement.

59 A strategic alliance is a co-operative business activity, formed by two or more separate organisations for strategic purposes. It involves forming a separate business entity, the shares of which are owned by two or more business entities.

Is this statement TRUE or FALSE?

A   True

B   False

SYLLABUS SECTION B: MANAGING THE FINANCE FUNCTION

60 Harry works in a large organisation which has both suppliers and customers all over the world. Harry is a CIMA qualified accountant and is responsible for managing foreign currency. In particular, Harry tries to minimise the company's exposure to foreign exchange losses.

What is Harry's role?

A   Treasurer

B   Management accountant

C   Financial accountant

D   Internal audit

61 **With regards to the management accounting function, which ONE of the following statements is correct?**

A   It is often used by external stakeholders, such as shareholders

B   It is a requirement for all limited companies

C   It is mainly a historic record of the organisation's activities

D   It aids planning and decision making within the business

62 K Co has recently split its accounting function into two parts – one that deals with management accounting and the other with financial accounting.

A   Management accounting

B   Financial accounting

Match the following statements to either A (management accounting) or B (financial accounting).

(i)   Preparation of the statement of profit or loss   B

(ii)   Recording of business transactions   B

(iii)   Preparation of statements for K Ltd's internal use   A

(iv)   No legal formats used   A

63 BB Co has recently reported a profit after tax figure for the year of $880,000. This is prior to preference dividends of $80,000 being deducted. The company has 100,000 shares in issue, 20% of which are preference shares.

The earnings per share (EPS) for the year is $ ⬚

64 **Which of the following functions is most likely to be undertaken in a treasury department?**

A   Preparation of cash flow statements

B   Foreign currency management

C   Product pricing decisions

D   Key factor analysis

65   **Which of the following statements regarding management accounting reports is correct?**

A   Budgets show the revenues and expenditure for the last accounting period.

B   Cost schedules are often also referred to as standard cost cards.

C   Variance reports compare the original budgets to revised budgets.

D   Management accountants will usually be responsible for creation of the statement of financial position.

66   **Which of the following statements regarding integrated reports is correct (select ALL that apply)?**

A   They involve the merging of the other financial statements to produce an overall view of company performance.

B   They are designed to show the organisation's profitability more clearly.

C   They include information on anything that is felt to be of interest to the users of the financial statements.

D   They include only relevant financial information for the users of the financial statements.

67   **Which ONE of the following is NOT one of the purposes of budgets?**

A   responsibility for expenditure

B   motivation of employees

C   co-ordination of staff

D   costing of units

68   Adrian works for VCF Co and has been asked to locate three pieces of information for his manager:

(1)   The total cost of making one unit of BH364 – VCF's only product.

(2)   The total equity of the company.

(3)   The difference between the original budget and actual results achieved in the last year.

Where would Adrian need to look for each of these pieces of information?

A   (1) Statement of profit or loss (SOPL) (2) Budget (3) Standard cost card

B   (1) Standard cost card (2) Statement of financial position (SOFP) (3) Variance report

C   (1) Statement of profit or loss (SOPL) (2) Statement of financial position (SOFP) (3) Budget

D   (1) Standard cost card (2) Statement of cash flows (3) Budget

69   Jared has recently placed some of his earnings into a scheme which is designed to reduce the amount of tax he pays to the Government. The scheme is legal, but a Government minister has described it as 'frustrating the intentions of Parliament'. The scheme is therefore an example of:

    A   Tax evasion

    B   Tax mitigation

    C   Tax avoidance

    D   Tax minimisation

70   S decided to record the purchases made on the 2nd of April 200X in tax year ending 31st of March 200X. The authorities will likely classify this as tax _____.

    Which of the following words correctly fill this gap?

    A   Evasion

    B   Minimisation

    C   Avoidance

    D   Suppression

71   **Tax mitigation involves which of the following?**

    A   Taking all legal steps to reduce one's tax liability

    B   Agreeing to pay a financial penalty to avoid prosecution

    C   Moving businesses and funds offshore to reduce liability to UK tax

    D   Reducing tax liabilities without frustrating the law makers' intentions

72   **An important advantage of using loans to finance investment is:**

    A   loan interest payments can usually be suspended if profits are low

    B   the timing of loan payments is often at the company's discretion

    C   loan interest is tax deductible

    D   banks will often not require security for loan advances

73   **Company G is considering raising finance to invest in new premises. It believes that it should raise debt finance by way of a bank loan. Which of the following statements are correct regarding debt and equity finance?**

    A   Interest payments tend to be cheaper than dividends

    B   Interest payments can be suspended in the future if H is unable to afford them

    C   Dividends are an allowable deduction against H's profits

    D   H will likely need to provide asset security to investors whether it chooses to raise debt or equity finance

74 VDF Co is planning to raise finance to fund the launch of a new product. It is planning to do this via an issue of new shares to the public. Which of the following is an issue that VDF may face if it proceeds with its plans to raise equity finance?

   A   It will be forced to pay higher dividends in the future – even if the new product launch is a failure

   B   The share issue may dilute the control that the existing shareholders have over the company

   C   VDF will require good quality assets to offer as security for the new issue

   D   The issue of shares is likely to reduce VDF's corporation tax liability

75 Working capital is calculated as:

   A   the excess of current assets over current liabilities

   B   the excess of bank borrowings over current assets

   C   the excess of long-term liabilities over short-term liabilities

   D   the excess of fixed assets over current assets

76 Al is trying to find certain key figures from the financial statements of HGF Co. In particular he needs to find:

   (1)   The net assets of HGF

   (2)   HGF's gross profit for the year

   (3)   HGF's share capital

   Al is unsure about whether to look at the Statement of Financial Position (SOFP) or the Statement or profit or loss (SOPL) for each one.

   Which of the following correctly matches the above items of information with the financial statements in which they would be found?

	(1)	(2)	(3)
A	SOFP	SOPL	SOPL
B	SOPL	SOFP	SOFP
C	SOPL	SOFP	SOPL
D	SOFP	SOPL	SOFP

77 The statement of profit or loss, the statement of financial position and the statement of cash flows are typically the only reports created by the financial accounting function.

   Is this statement TRUE or FALSE?

   A   True

   B   False

78   **E Co has a large marketing department. In which of the following ways would this department co-ordinate with E's accounting department?**

   A   Decisions on the quantity of raw materials required

   B   Establishing credit terms for customers

   C   Calculating pay rises for staff

   D   Decisions on the selling price of the product

79   **Which of the following is NOT a way in which an organisation's production department would co-ordinate with its accounting department?**

   A   Calculating charge out rates for services provided by the organisation

   B   Calculating the budgets for the number of units to be produced

   C   Estimation of the costs of the raw materials required for production

   D   Decisions on the quality of raw materials that the organisation can afford to use

80   **Below are a number of statements regarding internal and external audit. Which FOUR of the statements relate to internal audit rather than external?**

   A   It is a legal requirement for larger companies

   B   The scope of work is decided by management

   C   Can be undertaken by employees of the company

   D   Ultimately reports to the company's shareholders

   E   Reviews whether financial statements are true and fair

   F   Must be undertaken by independent auditors

   G   Mainly focuses on reviewing internal controls

   H   Ultimately reports to management

81   **The key purpose of internal auditing is to:**

   A   detect errors and fraud

   B   evaluate the organisation's risk management processes and systems of control

   C   give confidence as to the truth and fairness of the financial statements

   D   express an internal opinion on the truth and fairness of the financial statements

82   **Which THREE of the following are duties of the Company Secretary?**

   A   Identifying techniques for prioritising and managing risks

   B   Maintaining the company's statutory registers or books

   C   Reviewing internal controls

   D   Monitoring the organisation's cash balance and working capital

   E   Ensuring the security of the company's legal documents

   F   Filing annual returns at Companies House

83   A is preparing a seminar for the Board of Directors of the company she works for regarding internal and external audit and the differences between the two.

Which TWO of the following points are correct with regards to internal and external audit?

(i)   The scope of the internal auditors' work is determined by the management of the company, while external auditors determine the scope of their own work.

(ii)   Internal auditors test the organisation's underlying transactions, while external auditors test the operations of the organisation's systems.

(iii)   Internal audit and external audit are usually both legal requirements.

(iv)   Internal auditors can be employees of the company they audit, while external auditors must not be.

A   (i), and (ii) only

B   (i) and (iv) only

C   (ii) and (iv) only

D   (iii) and (iv) only

84   **Which of the following statements are correct with regards to external audit?**

(i)   Due to their in-depth examination of the business, external auditors are often able to provide advice to management on possible improvements to the business.

(ii)   External auditors often have an independence problem as they report to management and yet are also expected to give an objective opinion on them.

(iii)   External audits can help to resolve management disputes, such as disagreements over company valuations or profit-sharing agreements.

(iv)   External auditors have little or no interest in the internal controls of the organisation as these are the responsibility of the internal auditors.

A   (i) and (iii)

B   (i), (ii) and (iv)

C   (i), (iii) and (iv)

D   (ii) and (iv)

85   **Which of the following are considered to be the three prerequisites for fraud to occur?**

(1)   Motivation

(2)   Opportunity

(3)   Authority

A   (1) and (2)

B   (2) and (3)

C   (1) and (3)

D   (1), (2) and (3)

86 Consider the following two statements:

(1)   A comprehensive system of control will eliminate all fraud and error.

(2)   Employees working in departments other than Accounts have no responsibility for reporting fraud.

Which of these options is/are correct?

A   (1) only

B   (2) only

C   Both

D   Neither

87 **The finance function can be positioned in different ways within the organisation. When the finance function is carried out by an external party, this is known as:**

A   Shared Services Centres

B   Business Process Outsourcing

C   Business Partnering

D   Network organisation

88 The finance function can be positioned in three main ways:

Business partnering	Shared services centre (SSC)	Business process outsourcing (BPO)

Match the following definitions to the correct position above.

A   The finance function is carried out by an external party   *BPO*

B   A dedicated finance function is set up within each business unit   *BP*

C   The finance function is consolidated and run as a central unit within the organisation   *SSC*

89 MBK Co, a German based company, is considering moving some of its tasks to neighbouring Poland in order to reduce costs. This is an example of near-shoring.

Is this statement true or false?

A   True

B   False

90 **Which of the following shows the correct sequence for the stages of business process re-engineering (BPR)?**

A   Process identification, process redesign, process rationalisation, process reassembly

B   Process reassembly, process identification, process rationalisation, process redesign

C   Process identification, process reassembly, process rationalisation, process redesign

D   Process identification, process rationalisation, process redesign, process reassembly

SYLLABUS SECTION C: MANAGING TECHNOLOGY AND INFORMATION

91 Data is information that has been processed in such a way that it has meaning to the person who receives it.

Is this statement TRUE or FALSE?

A   True

B   False

92 **The outsourcing of an Information Technology service by an organisation can lead to which ONE of the following?**

A   Increased reliance on the IT department

B   Increased reliance on central departments generally

C   Certain staff having responsibility for monitoring contracts

D   Recruitment of additional programmers

93 **Identify THREE advantages of a pilot changeover.**

A   It is cheaper than a parallel changeover

B   It provides a degree of safety not offered by a direct changeover

C   It is easier to control than a parallel changeover

D   It is cheaper than a direct changeover

E   It provides a degree of safety not offered by a parallel changeover

94 **Which ONE of the following is the usual reason for dispersed and virtual team working in an organisation?**

A   Weak management

B   Utilisation of developments in technology and information systems

C   Poor hygiene factors in the workplace

D   Localised human resource management

95 **Electronic Executive Information Systems (EIS) and Expert Systems (ES) are examples of which ONE of the following?**

A   Customer relationship management software

B   Database management

C   Computer networking

D   Decision based software

96 **Which of the following are advantages of a database?**

A   The impact of systems failure is lower

B   Data accuracy is less important since the data is only held in one place

C   The information can be accessed in a flexible manner

D   Avoids data redundancy

E   Data integrity tends to be lower

97 **Corrective systems maintenance refers to which ONE of the following?**

A   A process undertaken prior to systems implementation

B   A remedy of defects after systems implementation

C   A process of upgrading both hardware and software

D   A means of ensuring that machines and equipment do not hold up production

98 **Which ONE of the following does NOT represent a control in a computer network?**

A   A firewall

B   Data encryption

C   Passwords

D   A cookie

99 **A software management system combining all of a globally diverse organisation's sales, marketing and customer support information is known as:**

A   distributed data processing (DDP)

B   customer relationship management (CRM)

C   a database management system (DBMS)

D   a wide area network (WAN)

100 **Information that takes the form of a list of debtors and creditors is by nature said to be:**

A   strategic

B   tactical

C   operational

D   executive

101   **Match the changeover methods in the list below to the relevant description.**

- Parallel
- Phased
- Direct
- Pilot

Method	Description
Phased	Involves gradual implementation of one sub-system at a time.
Parallel	The old system and the new system are both operated together for a while.
Pilot	Takes one whole part of the complete system and runs it as the new system. If this operates correctly then the remaining elements can be transferred gradually.
Direct	A switch to the new system and complete cessation of the old system at the same time.

102   **Presenting a new system with many unusual or unexpected events is an example of what type of testing?**

A   Contrived

B   Acceptance

C   Realistic

D   Adaptive

103   **Which ONE of the following is a program that impairs data and software?**

A   A virus

B   Corrective maintenance

C   Contrived testing

D   Cyber bullying

104   **IS client-vendor relationship is a feature of which ONE of the following?**

A   An outsourced IS function

B   Enterprise-wide systems

C   Social networking

D   Virtual team working

105 If an employee who is opposing the introduction of a new system is given a key role in its implementation, this is an example of which one of the following?

    A   Co-optation

    B   Career planning

    C   Succession planning

    D   Networking

106 Contrived, volume and realistic are examples of which one of the following?

    A   System testing methods

    B   Supply relationship categories

    C   Ways of classifying inventory

    D   Ways of estimating market potential

107 Which ONE of the following is NOT an example of a driving force in Lewin's force field analysis?

    A   Anxiety about job security

    B   Reduced running costs

    C   Improved information

    D   Fresh challenge in job

108 A post-implementation review is an important stage in the system changeover process.

    Is this statement TRUE or FALSE?

    A   True

    B   False

109 Local needs being taken into account and each office being more self-sufficient tend to be advantages of:

    A   outsourced information systems

    B   management information systems

    C   decentralised IS departments

    D   centralised IS departments

110 Corrective, adaptive and perfective are forms of:

    A   rewards and punishments used in people management

    B   performance management variables

    C   systems maintenance

    D   stock control methods

111   Data integrity and elimination of duplication are key features of:

    A   effective databases

    B   end user flexibility and autonomy

    C   autonomous (independent) working by different functions

    D   all social media tools

112   Which ONE of the following is NOT an approach to systems changeover?

    A   Parallel running

    B   Phased changeover

    C   Matrix operation

    D   Pilot testing

113   Which ONE of the following is NOT normally associated with outsourced IS solutions?

    A   Ensuring contract compliance

    B   Assembly and maintenance of a suitably skilled workforce

    C   Preparing formal tendering documents

    D   Invoicing, processing and payment

114   Technology which encourages user contributions and interactivity is known as:

    A   social media

    B   business 2 consumer (B2C)

    C   e-commerce

    D   teleworking

115   Which ONE of the following is NOT an IS outsourcing strategy?

    A   Ad hoc

    B   Total

    C   Project management

    D   Phased

116   Dispersed and virtual teams are normally a result of:

    A   an economic downturn

    B   developments in technology and information systems

    C   poor staff morale and motivation within the workforce

    D   ineffective human resource practices

117 Digital goods are any goods that are stored, delivered and used in an electronic format.

  Is this statement TRUE or FALSE?

  A   True

  B   False

118 Many large organisations have established a computer intranet for the purpose of:

  A   providing quick, effective and improved communication amongst staff using chat rooms

  B   providing quick, effective and improved communication to staff

  C   providing quick, effective and improved communication to customers

  D   providing quick, effective and improved ordering procedures in real time

119 Q Co is considering outsourcing its IT function to a third party IT company on a fixed fee basis. Q does not consider IT to be core function. A junior accountant has produced a list of possible advantages of this to the company. Which FOUR of the following factors are likely advantages of Q outsourcing its IT function?

  A   It will reduce the probability of other organisations gaining access to Q's information.

  B   It will reduce uncertainty relating to how much the IT function will cost Q each year.

  C   The third party company may have access to IT skills that Q lacks.

  D   If the third party fails to perform well, Q can easily bring the IT function back in-house.

  E   The third party company may have access to more economies of scale for IT, allowing Q to save money on its IT function.

  F   It will reduce Q's dependence on its suppliers.

  G   Q is likely to gain competitive advantage over rivals with its IT systems.

  H   It is likely to allow Q to focus its management time on core activities.

120 Which of the following would NOT be a potential disadvantage of forming a virtual company?

  A   A virtual company can look bigger than it actually is

  B   Quality may fall due to a loss of control

  C   The partners may also work for competitors

  D   It may be difficult for the partners to agree on how the revenue should be shared

121 The internet is an example of:

  A   parallel processing

  B   distributed processing

  C   a local area network

  D   a wide area network

122   Which ONE of the following technologies allows storage and accessing of data programs over the internet instead of on a computer's hard drive?

   A   Customer relationship management (CRM) systems

   B   Database management systems

   C   Cloud computing

   D   Knowledge management systems

123   Access to a larger market, targeted marketing, reduced costs and the elimination of intermediaries are just some of the benefits that could result from the implementation of:

   A   knowledge management systems

   B   e-commerce

   C   social media tools

   D   enterprise-wide systems

124   Which term is used to describe the 'deliberate accessing of on-line systems by unauthorised persons'?

   A   Hacking

   B   Human interference

   C   Virus attack

   D   Human resource risk

125   Which ONE of the following methods for overcoming resistance to a new system is most likely to use employee expertise?

   A   Education and communication

   B   Negotiation

   C   Facilitation and support

   D   Participation

126   Which ONE of the following factors is most likely to lead to successful organisational change?

   A   Imposed by external consultants

   B   Maintaining existing policies and procedures

   C   Autocratic leadership

   D   Initiated and supported by top management

127 Establishing a staff help line when attempting to cope with resistance to change is an example of:

A   facilitation

B   manipulation

C   coercion

D   co-optation

128 Which of the following statements relating to Big Data are true? Select ALL that apply.

A   Big Data refers to any financial data over $1 billion

B   The defining characteristics of Big Data are Velocity, Volume and Variety

C   Managing Big Data effectively can lead to increased competitive advantage

D   The term Big Data means 'data that comes from many sources'

E   Big Data contains both financial and non-financial data

129 F has recently started gathering extremely large volumes of information about his customers. His main concern is that his customers' details are changing rapidly and he is uncertain how to prevent his data becoming out of date.

Which ONE aspect of Gartner's 4Vs model is F having difficulties with?

A   Veracity

B   Velocity

C   Volume

D   Variety

130 Which THREE of the following are typical problems that organisations may face when dealing with Big Data?

A   The increasing use of electronic devices within society at large

B   A lack of skills in the labour pool relating to the handling of Big Data

C   Legal and privacy issues if data is held about individuals

D   Measurement of metrics that have no use to the organisation

E   Inability to monitor information from social media sites

SYLLABUS SECTION D: OPERATIONS MANAGEMENT

131 Which ONE of the following is NOT normally associated with Total Quality Management (TQM)?

  A   Six sigma

  B   5-S

  C   Kaizen

  D   Insourcing

132 The 4Vs of operations are variety, visibility, velocity and volume.

  Is this statement TRUE or False?

  A   True

  B   False

133 Diagrams which present the flow of information and products across supply networks are known as which ONE of the following?

  A   Process maps

  B   Fishbone 'cause and effect' diagrams

  C   Job analysis outlines

  D   Statistical control maps

134 The range of management issues associated with converting resources into required goods or services within an organisation is known as which ONE of the following?

  A   Sourcing strategies

  B   Product marketing

  C   Liberalisation

  D   Operations management

135 Which ONE of the following is NOT a category featured in Porter's Value Chain?

  A   Procurement

  B   Operations

  C   Marketing and sales

  D   Gross profit

136 The quality management thinker Philip Crosby is most closely associated with which ONE of the following ideas?

  A   Fitness for purpose

  B   The fishbone diagram

  C   Zero defects

  D   Business process re-engineering

137 **Which ONE of the following shows the correct sequence in the stages of product/service development?**

   A   Concept screening, consider customers' needs, design process, time-to-market, product testing

   B   Consider customers' needs, concept screening, design process, time-to-market, product testing

   C   Consider customers' needs, concept screening, design process, product testing, time-to-market

   D   product testing, time-to-market, consider customers' needs, concept screening, design process

138 **Most supply chains involve which ONE of the following?**

   A   A number of different companies

   B   An organisation's infrastructure

   C   After sales service

   D   A strategic apex

139 **Loss of goodwill and the expense of product recalls are known as which ONE of the following?**

   A   External failure costs

   B   Costs of lean

   C   Excess production costs

   D   Transaction costs

140 **A lean approach is associated with which ONE of the following?**

   A   Supply sourcing strategies

   B   Demographic profiling

   C   Employee selection criteria

   D   Removal of waste

141 **Under an ABC inventory management system which ONE of the following items should be monitored most closely?**

   A   'A' classified items

   B   'B' classified items

   C   'C' classified items

   D   All items equally

142 **Match the approaches to capacity planning in the list below to the relevant description.**

- Chase demand planning

- Level capacity planning

- Demand management planning

Approach	*Description*
demand	Aims to match production with demand.
chase	Attempts to influence demand to smooth variations above or below capacity.
level	Maintains production activity at a constant rate.

143 **Which ONE of the following is NOT a feature of a service?**

A   Intangibility

B   Immediate consumption

C   Inventory management

D   Involvement of the consumer

144 **Reck and Long's strategic positioning tool measures the contribution of which ONE of the following organisational functions?**

A   Quality control and assurance

B   Purchasing and supply

C   The management of systems

D   The management of human resources

145 **The aim of total productive maintenance is which ONE of the following?**

A   Inclusivity and empowerment

B   Motivation and teamwork

C   Engagement and commitment

D   Prevention and continuity

146 **Which ONE of the following does NOT represent a spoke in Cousins' supply wheel?**

A   Cost benefit analysis

B   Portfolio of relationships

C   Performance measures

D   A firm's infrastructure

147 Which THREE of the following are techniques used to forecast demand?

  A Regression analysis

  B Expert opinion polls

  C Statistical process control

  D Delphi technique

  E 5-s practice

148 Which ONE of the following is NOT normally associated with operations management?

  A Supply chain management

  B Enterprise Resource Planning systems

  C Liberalisation

  D Continuous inventory

149 What type of process technology can be used to control the exact movements of a machine allowing the creation of almost any desired pattern or shape?

  A Automated guided vehicles

  B Computer-integrated manufacturing

  C Flexible manufacturing systems

  D Computer numerical control

150 Which TWO of the following are features of a flexible manufacturing system?

  A Large batch production

  B The ability to change quickly from one job to another

  C Fast response times

  D Production line economies of scale

151 A 'fixed position' and 'cellular manufacturing' are two approaches to:

  A capacity planning

  B inventory management

  C layout

  D quality management

152 Which ONE of the following is NOT associated with quality improvement?

  A Fishbone diagrams

  B Pareto analysis

  C Five why analysis

  D Political lobbying

153 **Which ONE of the following is NOT an inventory management system?**

    A   Periodic

    B   EOQ

    C   ABC

    D   5S

154 **Supplier relationships in a supply network are categorised in which ONE of the following ways?**

    A   Single, multiple, delegated and parallel

    B   Primary, secondary and post-purchase

    C   Phased, pilot and integrated

    D   One-to-one, several to one, 180 degrees and 360 degrees

155 Taylor believed that an employee's main motivation is money.

Is this statement TRUE or FALSE?

    A   True

    B   False

156 **Which ONE of the following is NOT a cost of quality?**

    A   Internal failure

    B   Appraisal

    C   Prevention

    D   Transaction

157 **EOQ represents a form of:**

    A   inventory system based on economic order quantities

    B   European observance quality certification

    C   equal opportunity quantification index used in HRM

    D   Japanese inspired technique aimed at continuous improvement

158 **5S and 6 Sigma are examples of:**

    A   portfolio analysis frameworks

    B   marketing communication

    C   quality improvement practices

    D   Human Resource Development models

159   A key feature of a lean philosophy within operations is:

A   removal of waste

B   incremental change

C   official accreditation

D   continuous improvement

160   Small groups of employees that meet to identify work problems and their solution are known as:

A   quality circles

B   peer counsellors

C   cellular production teams

D   teleworkers

161   Porter's value system shows the organisation in terms of:

A   the value chains of suppliers, channels and the customer

B   primary activities, support activities and margin

C   the technostructure, strategic apex and operating core

D   passive, independent, supportive and integrative approaches to supply

162   Which ONE of the following is NOT associated with quality management?

A   5-S practice

B   180 degree feedback

C   Six Sigma methodology

D   Five-why process

163   Juran believed which ONE of the following?

A   That an organised, clean and standardised workplace is the key to quality management.

B   Managers should set up and then continually improve the systems in which people work.

C   Prevention of quality problems is key.

D   85% of quality problems are due to the systems that employees work within rather than the employees themselves.

164   Total productive maintenance involves:

A   maintaining worker satisfaction and high productivity

B   a cycle of PDCA

C   a prevention of quality failures through equipment faults

D   eliminating non-value adding activities from a process

165   The ABC system is a method of:

    A   managing inventory

    B   selection criteria

    C   production improvement

    D   quality compliance

166   A necessary product/service requirement to meet the Japanese interpretation of 'quality' is:

    A   to comply with all safety standards

    B   to cost no more than necessary

    C   to meet a design brief

    D   to meet customer expectations

167   Process design can be best improved by:

    A   an organisational restructure to reflect functions not processes

    B   improved checks on suppliers

    C   adopting a strategy of continuous improvement

    D   improved quality control

168   Collaborating with its suppliers may bring a company added value because it can:

    A   strike a harder bargain with its suppliers

    B   work with a supplier to improve quality and reduce costs

    C   avoid transaction costs

    D   introduce price competition amongst suppliers

169   Integrated solutions in product design and control of machinery are based on:

    A   a shared customer focused outlook

    B   a JIT philosophy

    C   CAD and CAM technologies

    D   decision support systems

170   Which TWO of the following are Kaizen tools?

    A   The fishbone diagram

    B   The five why process

    C   Cellular manufacturing

    D   Total productive maintenance

171   **Hammer and Champy identified the main themes of Business Process Re-engineering as:**

   A   process re-orientation, creative use of IT, ambition and rule-breaking

   B   effective process documentation, control and incentive bonus schemes

   C   documentation, a clear business ethos and an investment in training

   D   process review and enlightened HR practices

172   **Which of the following statements about MRP is correct?**

   A   MRP is a computer system that uses a database to integrate the systems for all functions within the organisation, such as operations management, engineering, sales and marketing and accounting.

   B   MRP ensures that inventory levels are maintained at sufficiently high levels to avoid the risk of 'stock-outs'.

   C   MRP is a computerised system for scheduling production based on economic batch quantities.

   D   MRP converts a master production schedule into production schedules for sub-assembly and parts and purchasing schedules for parts and raw materials.

173   **Which of the following statements about TQM is correct?**

   A   TQM relies on motivating employees to improve quality rather than on quality standards and statistical control methods.

   B   The level of defects must remain below a minimum acceptable level.

   C   All individuals within the organisation must be involved in quality improvements.

   D   The aim should be to eliminate all costs relating to quality.

174   **The Toyota Production System, from which the concept of lean manufacturing was derived, identified a number of types of waste in manufacturing. These included:**

   A   making defective products; motion; over-production

   B   motion; overspending; inventory and work-in-progress

   C   over-production; waste in processing; system defects

   D   waiting; human error; transportation

175   **A characteristic of lean manufacturing or a lean process is:**

   A   production initiated by 'supply push' rather than 'demand pull'

   B   large batch production

   C   small work cells

   D   workers with specific skills

176 **Which of the following is a concept in Just-in-Time production?**

A   The aim at all times should be to achieve maximum capacity utilisation of production resources.

B   It is better to have one large and complex machine than several small and simpler machines.

C   Set-up times should be increased.

D   The layout of a shop floor and the design of work flow can reduce production times.

177 **Which of the following approaches to operations management is inconsistent with the concept of continuous improvement?**

A   BPR

B   6 Sigma

C   Quality circles

D   5S

178 Reverse logistics involves disassembling a product and analysing its components and workings in detail.

Is this statement TRUE or FALSE?

A   True

B   False

179 The emergence of internet selling has increased the need for organisations to focus on their reverse logistics capability.

Is this statement TRUE or FALSE?

A   True

B   False

180 **Corrective work, the cost of scrap and materials lost are:**

A   examples of internal failure costs

B   examples of external failure costs

C   examples of appraisal costs

D   examples of preventative costs

181 **According to Porter's value chain, the final primary activity is referred to as:**

A   marketing and sales

B   outbound logistics

C   procurement

D   service

182   Supply chain partnerships grow out of:

A   quality accreditation

B   recognising the supply chain and linkages in a value system

C   an expansion of trade

D   adopting a marketing philosophy

SYLLABUS SECTION E: MARKETING

183   The terms 'guerrilla' and 'viral' are often applied to which ONE of the following?

A   Different organisational forms

B   Predatory take-over tactics

C   Marketing communications

D   Stakeholder groupings

184   When segmenting a market based on demographic factors, which ONE of the following would NOT be considered?

A   Age

B   Gender

C   Stage in the family life cycle

D   Frequency of purchase

185   Which ONE of the following is NOT normally associated with the decision making purchasing process?

A   Need recognition

B   Loyalty to a brand

C   Information searching

D   Post-purchase evaluation

186   Which ONE of the following is an example of secondary market research?

A   Telephone surveys to identify purchasing intentions

B   Focus group meetings to identify product preferences

C   Online questionnaires to identify buying habits

D   Use of search engines to identify market growth trends

187 An approach that encourages individuals to pass on a marketing message through existing social networks is known as:

A   guerrilla marketing

B   viral marketing

C   experiential marketing

D   cause marketing

188 An organisational approach that involves targeting an entire market with a single marketing mix is known as which ONE of the following?

A   Undifferentiated

B   Differentiated

C   Saturated

D   Blanket

189 The process of ensuring employees support an organisation's marketing activities is known as:

A   performance management marketing

B   social marketing

C   autocratic management

D   internal marketing

190 Which ONE of the following is NOT normally associated with an organisation's pricing mix?

A   Payment terms

B   Credit policy

C   Discounts for bulk purchase

D   Commission for a sales team

191 Which ONE of the following should logically precede market segmentation?

A   Market research

B   Targeting

C   Positioning

D   Promotional activity

192 In marketing the concept of 'physical evidence' refers to:

A   seeing the product before it is purchased

B   a physical meeting between vendor and buyer

C   some form of reassurance of service quality before purchase

D   proof that market research has actually been conducted

193 **Which ONE of the following is an example of a durable good?**

 A   Hand made shoes

 B   Long life milk

 C   Long lasting deodorant

 D   A jar of instant coffee

194 **In social marketing, goods that society discourages because of their negative social effects are known as which ONE of the following?**

 A   Demerit goods

 B   Durable goods

 C   International embargoes

 D   Imports

195 **For organisations failing to adopt the marketing philosophy, which ONE of the following is NOT recognised as an alternative?**

 A   Sales orientation

 B   Product orientation

 C   Lean orientation

 D   Production orientation

196 **Which ONE of the following is most likely to lead to an organisation accessing a larger market for its goods or services?**

 A   Cloud computing

 B   Teleworking

 C   e-trading

 D   Penetration marketing

197 **The extended marketing mix does NOT include which ONE of the following?**

 A   People

 B   Processes

 C   Physical evidence

 D   Positioning

198 **Which ONE of the following is an example of direct marketing?**

 A   Writing an article for a trade journal

 B   Targeting individual customers with promotional material

 C   Posting 'blogs' to draw attention to the organisation

 D   Public relations activities

199   Merit goods are commodities that:

A   comply with stringent international quality standards

B   society believes individuals should have for their wellbeing

C   are produced using expensive and highly valued ingredients

D   are earned through belonging to company loyalty schemes

200   The cognitive paradigm theory explains consumer behaviour through:

A   product branding

B   rational problem solving and decision making

C   past experience and levels of satisfaction

D   inertia or a lack of time

201   A manufacturer concerned mainly with production efficiencies and reducing unit costs is known as:

A   product orientated

B   production orientated

C   operationally strategic

D   a learning organisation

202   Consumer products which are not bought on a regular basis and are relatively expensive are known as:

A   durable goods

B   long term goods

C   luxury goods

D   fast moving consumer goods

203 **Match the marketing terms in the list below to the correct definitions.**

- Postmodern marketing
- Product orientation
- Relationship marketing
- Internal marketing

Term	Definition
	The technique of maintaining and exploiting the firm's customer base as a means of developing new business opportunities.
Relationship	A philosophical approach to marketing which focuses on giving the customer an experience that is customised to them and in ensuring they receive marketing messages in a form they prefer.
	A means of applying the philosophy and practices of marketing to the organisation's employees.
internal	The business centres its activities on continually improving and refining its products, assuming that customers simply want the best quality for their money.

204 With reference to marketing, the Ansoff matrix can assist in positioning.

Is this statement TRUE or FALSE?

A   True

B   False

205 **Which of the following is marketing or selling with a 'pull' effect?**

A   Placing products in display baskets in a supermarket, to encourage impulse buying

B   Offering a low price to a distributor to persuade him to stock the product

C   Direct selling by members of the sales team

D   Television advertising for a product

206 **Which of the following market research data-gathering techniques is most likely to be effective in estimating how many people buy a consumer product, in what quantities and how often?**

A   Sample surveys

B   Observation

C   Analysis of past sales for consumer products in total

D   Group interviewing

207 Which TWO of the following are NOT characteristics of service organisations?

    A   Homogenous products

    B   Inseparability of the service from the product

    C   Services are consumed immediately and cannot be stored

    D   Services are intangible

    E   Services result in the transfer of property

208 Which ONE of the following is the most suitable definition of internal marketing?

    A   Marketing the organisation's products to its own employees.

    B   Training employees who deal with customers (either directly or indirectly) to provide customer satisfaction in the work they do.

    C   Marketing activities carried on from the organisation's own premises, such as direct mail activities and telemarketing.

    D   Training employees in the features of the products and services sold by the organisation.

209 Analysing a market into sub-groups of potential customers with common needs and behaviours in order to target them through marketing techniques is called:

    A   market research

    B   market development

    C   segmentation

    D   product adaptation

210 The decision making unit includes separate people or groups who are all involved in a buying decision. Which ONE of the following is NOT part of the decision making unit?

    A   Gatekeepers

    B   Approvers

    C   Sellers

    D   Deciders

211 Public relations activity can be used within marketing as part of:

    A   marketing decision support activities

    B   a promotional mix

    C   customer feedback processes

    D   segmentation practices

212 The pricing strategy which involves charging a very low price when a new product is first introduced to gain rapid growth in market share is:

    A   market penetration

    B   loss leader pricing

    C   product penetration

    D   skim pricing

213 The use of 'skim pricing' as a marketing technique will result in:

    A   non-recovery of promotional costs

    B   enticing new customers to buy a product or service

    C   high prices normally at an early stage of the product lifecycle

    D   low prices so denying competitors opportunities to gain market share

214 Undifferentiated market positioning involves the targeting of:

    A   a single market segment with a single marketing mix

    B   a single market segment ignoring the concept of the marketing mix

    C   an entire market with a different marketing mix for each segment

    D   an entire market with a single marketing mix

215 Direct mailing, branding activities and public relations campaigns are all examples of:

    A   market processes

    B   product placement

    C   promotion

    D   market research

216 Selling products at a loss in order to generate more sales of other products is referred to as:

    A   loss leader pricing

    B   opportunistic pricing

    C   penetration pricing

    D   predatory pricing

217 The product life cycle is depicted on a chart or diagram as a line against the variables of:

    A   cash flow and market share

    B   number of customers and sales value

    C   sales volume and time

    D   relative market share and market growth rate

218   A company that concentrates on product features it instinctively believes to be "right" is referred to as:

   A   a learning organisation

   B   production orientated

   C   product orientated

   D   early stage entrepreneurial

219   In the Boston Consulting Group matrix, a question mark relates to a product with low market growth and high market share.

   Is this statement TRUE or FALSE?

   A   True

   B   False

220   **Which FOUR of the following are features of business to business (B2B) marketing?**

   A   Many buyers compared to business to consumer marketing

   B   High purchasing power of each buyer

   C   A close relationship between buyers and sellers in common

   D   Fewer buyers than business to consumer marketing

   E   Derived demand

   F   Low purchasing power of each buyer

SYLLABUS SECTION F: MANAGING HUMAN RESOURCES

221   Personal characteristics, qualifications and necessary experience expected of a particular post holder are normally all found in which ONE of the following documents?

   A   Job description

   B   Person specification

   C   Reference letter

   D   Summary appraisal meeting record

222   The psychological contract is an important factor when considering which ONE of the following?

   A   Staff retention

   B   Supply networks

   C   Buyer behaviour

   D   Corporate political activity

223 **Assessment centres are associated with which ONE of the following activities?**

    A   Staff selection

    B   Career counselling

    C   Focus group market research

    D   Societal marketing

224 **An assessment centre commonly refers to which ONE of the following?**

    A   A building where testing occurs

    B   An approach to selection

    C   An approach to recruitment

    D   Online supplier vetting procedure

225 **The basis of a psychological contract is:**

    A   an understanding of mutual obligations between a worker and the organisation

    B   a corporate responsibility to act in a way that does not harm the environment

    C   an emotional affinity for a particular product brand

    D   an organisation-wide commitment to listen to customer views

226 Personnel views employees as assets and motivates them by payment and coercion whereas human resource management (HRM) views employees as costs and motivates them by consent and involvement.

    Is this statement TRUE or FALSE?

    A   True

    B   False

227 **The Guest model of HRM contains six components. Choose THREE of these components from the list below.**

    A   Behavioural outcomes

    B   HRM theories

    C   Social outcomes

    D   HRM strategy

    E   HRM tactics

    F   Financial outcomes

228 A recruitment and training plan may be created as part of stage 4 of the HR plan 'put plans in place to close the gap'.

    Is this statement TRUE or FALSE?

    A   True

    B   False

229 Cattell's 16PF test is normally associated with which ONE of the following?

A   IS feasibility studies

B   The process of market segmentation

C   Auditing existing supply arrangements

D   Employee selection

230 Match the stage of the HR cycle below with the correct description.

- Appraisal

- Training

- Development

- Selection

Stage	Description
Selection	Choosing the best person for the job from a field of candidates sourced via recruitment.
Appraisal	Systematic review and assessment of an employee's performance, potential and training needs.
Training	Formal learning to achieve the level of skills, knowledge and competence to carry out the current role.
Develop	Realisation of a person's potential through formal and informal learning to enable them to carry out their current and future role.

231 Which ONE of the following is associated with recruitment rather than selection?

A   Assessment centres

B   Interviews

C   Advertising copy

D   Psychometric testing

232 The use of assessment centres and psychometric tests is normally associated with processes of:

A   recruitment

B   selection

C   induction

D   appraisal

233 CIMA's Code of Ethics for professional accountants is based upon:

A   a framework of fundamental principles

B   a framework of strict rules

C   a scale of penalties for non-compliance

D   sustainability principles and best practice

234 **David Kolb identified a four stage model representing:**

A   a quality evaluation framework

B   a cycle of learning from experience

C   a career planning and development framework

D   a way of assessing the value of training events

235 **James has just attended an interview for the post of accounting assistant at GB Co. A number of people interviewed James simultaneously. What type of interview was this?**

A   Stress

B   Tandem

C   Sequential

D   Panel

236 **Which TWO of the following are types of testing used as part of the selection process?**

A   Psychometric

B   Sequential

C   Contrived

D   Aptitude

E   Realistic

237 **Charles Handy's vision of a 'shamrock' organisation suggests a workforce that comprises three different type of worker, namely:**

A   strategic, operational and support

B   qualified, trainee and unskilled

C   'white collar', 'blue collar' and e-worker

D   core, contractual and flexible labour

238 **The set of activities designed to familiarise a new employee with an organisation is called:**

A   job analysis

B   induction

C   selection

D   manipulation and co-optation

239 **Recruitment involves:**

A   advertising a vacancy and interviewing

B   conducting interviews and tests

C   advertising a vacancy and initial screening of candidates

D   ensuring that contract negotiation complies with organisational policy

240   **An effective appraisal system involves:**

   A   assessing the personality of the appraisee

   B   a process initiated by the manager who needs an update from the appraisee

   C   advising on the faults of the appraisee

   D   a participative, problem-solving process between the manager and appraisee

241   A competency framework should regularly be updated by the employee to assess whether they still have the appropriate skills and abilities needed for their role.

   Is this statement TRUE or FALSE?

   A   True

   B   False

242   **Selection tests that fail to produce similar results over time when taken by the same candidate are:**

   A   contradictory

   B   unreliable

   C   too general

   D   unstable

243   **Why is succession planning desirable in a large organisation?**

   A   To ensure that promotion opportunities exist

   B   To ensure business continuity

   C   To ensure competence in key functions

   D   To prevent natural wastage of staff

244   **When it wishes to appoint full-time office staff, a company might use the services of an employment agency for:**

   A   recruitment and selection only

   B   recruitment and screening only

   C   screening and selection only

   D   screening only

245   **In which of the following situations is it most likely that an unfair dismissal has occurred?**

   A   An employee leaves his job claiming that the employer was in breach of contract by demoting him

   B   The employer terminates a fixed term contract with a sub-contractor without notice

   C   The employer dismisses a lorry driver who has been banned from driving by the court

   D   The employer dismisses an employee because of redundancy

246 **What is the major difficulty in establishing a basic pay structure for knowledge work?**

   A   Job evaluation

   B   Benchmarking

   C   Scarcity of individuals with knowledge skills

   D   Performance evaluation

247 **Andrea has just attended her appraisal with her line manager. She felt that the feedback was poorly delivered and that the manager viewed it purely as a form filling exercise. Which TWO of Lockett's barriers to effective appraisal may have been present here?**

   A   Chat, bureaucracy

   B   Confrontation, unfinished business

   C   Chat, judgement

   D   Confrontation, bureaucracy

248 **What is the main practical reason for asking an applicant for a reference from a former employer, as part of the selection process for a vacant job?**

   A   To gain another person's opinion about the suitability of the candidate for the job

   B   To find out whether the candidate has any personal faults or weaknesses

   C   To assess what the candidate's future performance in the job might be

   D   To establish whether the candidate has been telling the truth about his previous employment history

249 **The purpose of job evaluation is to:**

   A   assess the personal qualities required to do the job

   B   assess what the responsibilities of the job should be

   C   assess the performance of the job holder

   D   assess a fair rate of pay for the job

250 **Performance-related pay involves:**

   A   rewarding employees with a proportion of total profits

   B   rewarding employees with a proportion of total profits in excess of a target minimum level

   C   rewarding employees on the basis of the amount of work they have done

   D   rewarding employees for achieving agreed personal targets

251 Activities aimed at attracting a number of suitable candidates interested in joining an organisation are called:

A   human relationship marketing

B   recruitment

C   selection

D   human capital harvesting

252 Match the learning styles below with the correct explanation.

- Pragmatist

- Activist

- Reflector

- Theorist

Learning style	Explanation
Pragmatist	Adapt and integrate information in a step-by-step logical way.
Reflector	Prefer to step back to ponder and observe others before taking action.
Theorist	Are keen to try out new ideas, theories and techniques to see if they work in practise.
Activist	Involve themselves fully and without bias in new experiences.

253 Which of the following HR activities should be the most difficult to outsource to an external organisation?

A   Staff development

B   Relocation

C   Training

D   Recruitment

254 In terms of employment CIMA's Ethical Guidelines require members to:

A   act responsibly in the way that all other professionals do

B   act responsibly but in a way that satisfies organisational demands and pressures

C   act responsibly but in a way that satisfies the individual's own ethical code

D   act responsibly, honour any legal contract of employment and conform to employment legislation

255 **Kirkpatrick suggested a model for training evaluation that contains four levels. Which sequence shows the levels in the correct order from 1 to 4?**

    A   Results, reaction, learning, behaviour

    B   Reaction, learning, behaviour, results

    C   Behaviour, reaction, results, learning

    D   behaviour, results, reaction, learning

256 **Equal opportunities and diversity in the workplace are often confused. Which of the following relates to diversity?**

    A   Its purpose is to remove discrimination

    B   It relies on proactive action

    C   It is a Human Resources role

    D   It is a managerial role

257 **Which of the following would be a justified reason for redundancy?**

    A   Where an employee's conduct is unacceptable

    B   Where a department or team persistently underperforms

    C   Where an employee is no longer legally able to perform the role

    D   Where an employee's part of the business ceases trading

Section 2

ANSWERS TO OBJECTIVE TEST QUESTIONS

SYLLABUS SECTION A: INTRODUCTION TO ORGANISATIONS

1   D

Organisations do not have to create a product or service in order to be classified as an organisation. For example, an orchestra may be classed as an organisation, but it does not necessarily create a product.

2   A

'Schools' is the correct answer because the other organisations are normally found in the private (i.e. non-governmental) sector.

3   C

C is the correct answer because this is the main activity in the public sector. Options A and B relate to the private sector and D to a mutual organisation.

4   C

This is the definition of the term 'synergy'. Note that organisations may also allow specialisation, meaning that individuals can focus on becoming highly skilled in just one area.

5   A

As public limited companies are able to sell their shares to the public, they will often find it easier to raise large amounts of capital for growth, if needed. This may be much harder for partnerships and sole traders. Only public companies can sell shares to the public, companies may be owned by only one shareholder and shareholders enjoy limited liability.

6   A

A limited company has a separate legal personality from its owners.

7   C

Partnerships and companies would both usually be profit seeking. While government departments are likely to be not-for-profit, they would be part of the public sector. Therefore only charities would be likely to be both public AND not-for-profit.

8   C

Co-operatives are organised solely to meet the needs of the member-owners. Non-governmental organisations (NGOs) do not have profit as a primary goal and are not linked to national governments. Charities may be examples of NGOs. Private limited companies have shareholders, not members.

9   C

A limited liability company is classed as a separate legal entity from its owners. The owners (shareholders) may be different to the managers (Board of Directors). A shareholder's liability is limited to their investment.

A partnership is different to a limited company in that there is no separate legal entity.

Sole traders have unlimited liability for business debts as they are classed as the same legal entity as the business.

There is no restriction on the number of partners in a partnership agreement

10   C AND E

A NGO is a private organisation that pursues activities to relieve suffering, promote the interests of the poor, protect the environment, provide basic social services or undertake community development. Given this it is unlikely that a NGO would seek to make a profit.

As the name would suggest, non-governmental organisations are not funded by government.

11   B

By definition.

12   B

Because the entrepreneurial structure is run by one person who makes all the decisions, this powerful individual will have strong control over the organisation and its strategic direction, leading to better goal congruence.

13   D

Function managers may make decisions to increase their own power, or in the interests of their own function, rather than in the interests of the company overall. Economies of scale, standardisation and specialists feeling comfortable are advantages of a functional structure.

14   C

A matrix structure aims to combine the benefits of decentralisation (e.g. speedy decision making) with those of co-ordination. The more rigid structure in a divisional company would not have the necessary flexibility.

15   D

A refers to an entrepreneurial structure.

B is typical of a functional structure.

C describes a divisional structure.

In a matrix structure individuals will have dual command, a functional manager and a divisional manager. This can cause conflict between departments and stress for the individual.

16   C and D

The first two features relate to a functional structure.

17   A

If H wants to manage each product separately, it will need to adopt either a matrix or divisional approach, as these would allow the creation of separate divisions for each product. However, H wishes to keep its administrative costs as low as possible. As the matrix structure has high admin costs due to high numbers of managers, A should adopt a divisional approach.

18   D

The granting of authority over each geographic area to geographic bosses results in a potential loss of control over key operating decisions. This weakness is also present in the Product/Division/Department structure.

19   A

The span of control is the number of people for whom a manager is directly responsible.

Scalar chain relates to the number of management levels within an organisation.

20   A

A wide span of control means that each manager looks after many staff members. This is easier if the staff members are skilled and motivated as they will require little supervision. However, if staff are widely spread or have to undertake complex tasks, it will be harder for a manger to look after them meaning that the span of control will tend to narrow.

21   C

By definition. Hollow organisations outsource non-core functions, while virtual organisations outsource almost all functions – whether core or not. Entrepreneurial is not a type of boundaryless structure.

22   A

When outsourcing, transaction costs arise from the effort that must be put into specifying what is required and subsequently co-ordinating delivery and monitoring quality.

23   C

When outsourcing, transaction costs arise from the effort that must be put into specifying what is required and subsequently co-ordinating delivery and monitoring quality.

24

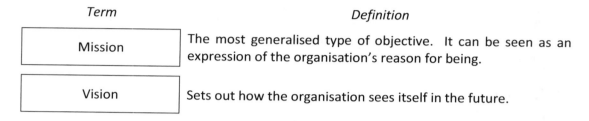

Term	Definition
Mission	The most generalised type of objective. It can be seen as an expression of the organisation's reason for being.
Vision	Sets out how the organisation sees itself in the future.

25   D

By definition.

26   C

Offshoring is the relocation of corporate activities to a foreign country.

27   A

Transaction costs are the indirect costs (i.e. the non-production costs) incurred in performing a particular activity, for example the expenses incurred through outsourcing.

28   D

A service level agreement (SLA) sets out the terms and conditions of the outsourcing arrangement and should be drawn up between the client and the supplier.

29   C

Offshoring is the relocation of corporate activities to a foreign country.

30   C

Transaction costs are the expenses incurred by allowing some activity to be undertaken outside the organisation, e.g. through outsourcing. Answer A, externalities, are the costs/benefits of production experienced by society but not by consumers/producers. Answer B, uncertainty costs is a made up term. Answer D, internal failure costs, are a type of quality cost.

31   B, F, G and H

32   D

Reasons for the separation of ownership and control include the suggestion that specialist management can run the business better than those who own the business.

33   A

34   C

The government has high power and low interest. Mendelow would therefore suggest that it needs to be kept satisfied.

35   C

By definition.

36   C and D

A non-executive director must not have been an employee of the organisation in the last five years and should not have had a **material** business interest in the company in the last three years. They should also not participate in the company's share options or pension schemes or hold cross directorship (i.e. two or more directors sit on the board of the same third part company).

37   A

A is correct – in smaller companies there should be at least two non-executives. They are not involved in the day-to-day running of the company and should have no links to the executive directors, as this may impair their independence. In addition, they should not act for a prolonged period of time as this may also impair their independence.

38   A

Out of the list given, only A comprises board members.

39   D

Lobbyists will seek to put their case to the government to influence legislative or regulative processes. Therefore, lobbying is an example of political activity.

40   A

By definition.

41   C

Corporate political activity (CPA) refers to the involvement of firms in the political process, with the aim of securing particular policy preferences.

42   A

By definition.

43   D

Answer D is not a benefit of corporate governance since corporate governance is the set of processes and policies by which the **company** is directed, administered and controlled and will therefore not prevent fraudulent claims by an external party, i.e. contractors. Answer A is a benefit since good governance will result in a better image with the providers of finance thus making raising finance easier. Answer B is also a benefit since good governance should result in sustainable wealth creation. Answer C is a benefit since customers will prefer to purchase a product or service from a company that has a strong reputation for good governance and hence lower levels of risk.

44   A

By definition.

45   C

A closed system is closed off from the outside environment and all interaction and knowledge is transmitted within the closed system only. Attention is focused on the refinement of the existing structure, the wider context is taken as given. A machine bureaucracy is an example of a closed system, holding efficiency and control as the highest goals.

46   A

Regulation is any form of government interference and is required to ensure that the needs of stakeholders can be met and that businesses act in the public interest. For regulation to be efficient the total benefit to the nation must be greater than the total cost.

47   A

Other than political lobbying, there is little that most firms can do to influence external environmental issues.

48   D

Directors, who are placed in control of resources that they do not own and are effectively agents of the shareholders. They should be working in the best interests of the shareholders. However, they may be tempted to act in their own interests, for example by voting themselves huge salaries. The background to the agency problem is the separation of ownership and control – in many large companies the people who own the company (the shareholders) are not the same people as those who control the company (the board of directors).

49   B

Sustainable development focuses on meeting the needs of the present without compromising the ability of future generations to meet their own needs.

50   D

A negative externality is an adverse social consequence which the private producer has no incentive to minimise.

51   B

Only if they are part of a US listed company are UK listed companies affected by Sarbanes Oxley.

52   ALL OF THEM

All of the above would raise ethical issues. Materials used impacts on the safety of the product. Quality is potentially a safety issue. Advertising raises issues of truth and manipulation. The treatment and potential exploitation of labour, whether directly employed by a business or its suppliers, is also an ethical issue.

53   A and C

CSR is likely to attract good quality employees and should not lead to a loss of key skills within the organisation. However, goods need to be purchased from ethical sources, which may lead to a rise in their cost. It can also take up significant amounts of management time, which could have been used to increase business profits.

54   A, B and C

Ensuring sustainability may require a significant amount of management time and attention, which is unlikely to reduce their administrative burden. Options A, B and C would, however, be typical benefits of such an approach.

55   A, D and E

Improved consistency of service, systems consolidation and cost savings are all potential advantages of a shared service approach. Answer B is incorrect since more resources will be required to migrate diverse systems. Answer C is also incorrect since a shared service approach is not necessarily favourable to outsourcing.

56   B

While all four options would improve the overall environmental impact of the company, only option B would actually reduce the amount of wastage of G itself. By trying to predict demand accurately, the company can make only as much G as is needed, thereby reducing wastage.

57   B

Mintzberg's effective organisation is made up of the strategic apex, middle line, operating core, technostructure and support staff.

58

Principle	Interpretation
Professional competence and due care	Maintaining a relevant level of professional knowledge and skills so that a competent service can be provided.
Professional behaviour	Complying with relevant laws and regulations.
Integrity	Being straightforward, honest and truthful in all professional and business relationships.
Confidentiality	Not disclosing information unless there is specific permission or a legal or professional duty to do so.
Objectivity	Not allowing bias, conflict of interest or the influence of other people to override professional judgement.

59   B – FALSE

A strategic alliance is a co-operative business activity, formed by two or more separate organisations for strategic purposes. However, it does not involve forming a separate business entity, the shares of which are owned by two or more business entities (this would relate to a joint venture).

SYLLABUS SECTION B: MANAGING THE FINANCE FUNCTION

60   A

The treasury department will monitor foreign exchange and try to minimise the company's exposure to foreign exchange losses.

61   D

The other three are correct for financial accounting.

62   (i)   B

(ii)   **B**

(iii)   **A**

(iv)   **A**

63   10

EPS = PAT (less pref divs)/weighted average number of ordinary shares in issue.

= ($880,000 – $80,000)/(100,000 × 80%)

= $10

64   B

While treasurers will deal with cash management (amongst other things) they do not produce cash flow statements – this is part of the role of a financial accounting function. C and D would both be undertaken by a management accountant.

65   B

Budgets lay out the planned income and expenditure for the coming period. Variance reports compare actual results to the budget for a period. The statement of financial position is the responsibility of financial accountants.

66   C ONLY

Integrated reports will provide users with additional information on anything the organisation feels they would be interested in, such as the company's environmental impact or sustainability in the period.

67   D

Costing of units would the purpose of a cost schedule or standard cost card.

68   B

Make sure you are able to identify the contents of the main financial and management reports produced by the accounts department.

69   C

Tax evasion is illegal. Tax avoidance is used to describe schemes that frustrate the intentions of Parliament, while tax mitigation describes schemes that do not frustrate the intentions of Parliament. Tax minimisation is a made up term.

70   A

This is tax evasion as the company is illegally reducing its tax liability. Note that it cannot be both evasion AND avoidance simultaneously.

71   D

Tax avoidance is used to describe schemes which, whilst they are legal, are designed to defeat the intentions of the law makers. Thus, once a tax avoidance scheme becomes public knowledge, the law makers will usually step in to change the law to stop the scheme from working.

72   C

A, B and D are not true. They describe advantages of using the issue of share capital to finance investment.

73   A

Interest tends to be cheaper than dividends. However, a company cannot normally suspend debt repayments if it can no longer afford them – this is only possible with dividends. Dividends are not an allowable deduction, but interest is. Finally, shareholders would not normally receive any security on their investment, meaning that D is also incorrect.

74   B

A is incorrect as VDF will never have to pay dividends if it cannot afford them. Equity finance is not secured on the company's assets, so C is incorrect. D is also incorrect as dividends are not tax allowable, meaning that the issue of shares is unlikely to directly affect VDF's tax liability.

75   A

Working capital is the capital available for conducting the day-to-day operations of an organisation.

76   D

Remember that the SOFP shows the assets, liabilities and capital of the company, while the SOPL shows the income and expenses (and therefore the profit or loss) of the business in the period.

77   B – FALSE

Others include the sustainability and integrated reports.

78   D

The accounting department can help ensure a profitable selling price is used for E's products.

79   A

Option A would most likely be a marketing or service provision crossover with the accounting department.

80   B, C, G and H

81   B

The internal audit also makes recommendations for the achievement of company objectives.

C is the role of the external auditors.

82   B, E and F

Maintaining the company's statutory registers or books, ensuring the security of the company's legal documents and filing annual returns at Companies House are all duties of the company secretary. Answers A (identifying techniques for prioritising and managing risks) and C (reviewing internal controls) are functions of internal audit whereas answer D (monitoring the organisation's cash balance and working capital) is one of the roles of the treasury function.

83   B

Statement (ii) is the wrong way round – external auditors test the underlying transactions that make up the financial statements, while internal auditors test the operations of the company's systems. Statement (iii) is also incorrect as internal audit is not usually a legal requirement, though corporate governance principles state that if an internal audit function is not present, the company should annually assess the need for one.

84   A

Statement (ii) is incorrect as this issue of independence would normally be an issue for internal auditors – not external auditors. Statement (iv) is also incorrect as, if the internal controls are reliable, it will reduce the amount of substantive testing that the external auditor is required to perform.

85   A

The third prerequisite is dishonesty. An honest employee is unlikely to commit fraud even if given the opportunity and motive.

86   D

In practice many organisations find that fraud is impossible eradicate. With regards to error, as it is unintentional, it will be hard to prevent such mistakes from taking place.

In addition, there is an implied duty within an employment contract so as to encourage staff to be honest and report any actual or suspected fraud.

87   B

Business process outsourcing is where the finance function is outsourced and carried out by an external party. This can bring a number of benefits to the organisation, including cost reduction, best practice and it can release capacity within the organisation to allow the retained finance staff to concentrate on more value-adding activities.

Shared services centres are where the finance function is consolidated and run as a central unit within the organisation.

Business partnering is where the finance function is embedded within the business area which it supports.

A network organisation is 'a series of strategic alliances that an organisation creates with suppliers, manufacturers and distributors to produce and market a product' (Lysons and Farrington).

88   B, C, A

B = Business partnering	C = Shared services centre (SSC)	A = Business process outsourcing (BPO)

89   A – TRUE

Near-shoring means that the company moves its tasks overseas but to a neighbouring country.

90   D

The stages of BPR are process identification, process rationalisation, process redesign, process reassembly.

SYLLABUS SECTION C: MANAGING TECHNOLOGY AND INFORMATION

91   B – FALSE

The statement is false – information is data that has been processed in such a way that it has meaning to the person who receives it. Data, on the other hand, are facts or figures in a raw, unprocessed format.

92   C

All the others are consequences of in-house IT services.

93   A, B and C

A pilot changeover tends to be cheaper and easier to control than a parallel changeover (answers A and C) and it will provide a degree of safety not offered by a direct changeover (answer B). However, it will not be cheaper than a direct changeover (answer D) and the degree of safety offered will be less than when using a parallel changeover (answer E).

94   B

Virtual team working is increasing due to developments in technology.

95   D

The primary purpose of EIS and ES (types of management information system) are to help managers make decisions.

96   C, D

Databases allow flexible access to information and avoid data redundancy (duplication). The other answers are incorrect since the impact of system failure is **higher** (answer A), data accuracy is **more** important (answer B) and data integrity tends to be **higher** (answer E).

97   B

Corrective maintenance corrects technical difficulties that have arisen in the operation of the system. It is the final step of the SDLC and occurs after systems implementation.

98   D

A cookie measures how consumers use a website so that it can be updated and improved based on consumer needs. It is not a type of control in a computer network.

99   B

By definition.

100 C

Operational information is used to ensure routine tasks are properly planned and controlled. A list of debtors and creditors is an example of operational data.

101

Method	Description
Phased	Involves gradual implementation of one sub-system at a time.
Parallel	The old system and the new system are both operated together for a while.
Pilot	Takes one whole part of the complete system and runs it as the new system. If this operates correctly then the remaining elements can be transferred gradually.
Direct	A switch to the new system and complete cessation of the old system at the same time.

102 A

By definition. Answers B and C are other types of system testing. Answer D is a type of system maintenance.

103 A

By definition.

104 A

The clue is in the word 'vendor' suggesting outsourcing.

105 A

By definition.

106 A

Contrived, volume and realistic are examples of system testing methods, the other main one being 'acceptance testing'.

107 A

Anxiety about job security (answer A) may act as a restraining force which will push back to the current state, i.e. continuing to use the current system.

108 B – FALSE

A post-implementation review is part of the systems evaluation.

109 C

A decentralised IS involves functions being spread out throughout the organisation meaning that local needs are taken into account and offices tend to be more self sufficient.

110 C

Corrective, adaptive and perfective are the three forms of systems maintenance.

111 A

A database should result in reduced duplication of data and increased data integrity.

112 C

A matrix operation is a form of organisational structure. There are four approaches to systems implementation; direct, parallel, pilot and phased.

113 B

The assembly and maintenance of a suitably skilled workforce would usually be carried out by the third party that the company outsources its IS solutions to.

114 A

Facebook, Twitter and Youtube are well-known examples of social media interactivity.

115 D

Phased (answer D) is a type of system changeover. Ad hoc, project management, partial and total are the four types of IS outsourcing strategy.

116 B

Developments in technology and information systems have allowed people who are not present in the same office to work together as a team.

117 A – TRUE

By definition – digital goods are any goods that are stored, delivered and used in an electronic format.

118 B

An intranet is an internal network within an organisation that makes use of the internet. It can be used for communications to employees and also between employees. However, e-mail is used for communications between employees within an intranet, not chat rooms.

119 B, C, E and H

120   A

This is an advantage of being a virtual company. Virtual companies can be made to look much bigger than they actually are, enabling them to compete with large and successful organisations. Answers B, C and D are all potential disadvantages of forming virtual companies.

121   D

A wide area network (WAN) can link computers in different geographical locations or organisations. The internet is an example of a WAN.

122   C

By definition – cloud computing allows storage and access of data programs over the internet instead of on a computer's hard drive.

123   B

E-commerce refers to the conducting of business electronically via some sort of communications link and may result in access to larger markets, targeted marketing, reduced costs and elimination of intermediaries.

124   A

Hacking is the term used to describe the deliberate accessing of on-line systems by unauthorised persons.

125   D

The participation of employees in the change process has the advantage of utilising their expertise.

126   D

A change culture within an organisation has to start with top management, who must give their full support and encouragement to change programmes. Answer B implies no change at all. Attempts to impose change are likely to end in failure and therefore answers A and C are both incorrect.

127   A

The help-line is to assist staff, not to coerce or manipulate them, and has little to do with co-optation.

128   B, C and E

Option A is incorrect in that Big Data does not refer to any specific financial amount. Option D is also incorrect. Big Data can indeed come from many sources, but this is too narrow a definition. Big Data refers to the large volume of data, the many sources of data and the many types of data.

129 B

The data is changing with great velocity (speed) which may be making it difficult for F to keep his information up to date.

130 B, C AND D

Note that the increasing use of electronic devices makes Big Data collection easier. Many organisations successfully gather information from social media sites such as Facebook and Twitter and use it to great effect within their decision-making processes.

SYLLABUS SECTION D: OPERATIONS MANAGEMENT

131 D

Six sigma, 5S and Kaizen are all common within TQM environments.

132 B – FALSE

The 4Vs of operations are variety, visibility, variation and volume. Velocity is one of the characteristics of Big Data.

133 A

By definition.

134 D

By definition.

135 D

The value chain looks at activities not outcomes.

136 C

Make sure you learn the detail regarding different writers on quality.

137 B

The correct sequence in the stages of product/ service development is consider customers' needs, concept screening, design process, time-to-market, product testing.

138 A

Most companies outsource at least part of their supply chain.

139 A

By definition.

140   D

Lean management is a philosophy that aims to systematically reduce waste.

141   A

ABC divides an organisation's inventory into different classifications – A, B or C. Managers focus on 'A' items. These are items of high value in terms of usage rate.

142

Approach	Description
Chase demand planning	Aims to match production with demand.
Demand management planning	Attempts to influence demand to smooth variations above or below capacity.
Level capacity planning	Maintains production activity at a constant rate.

143   C

Services are consumed immediately and cannot be stored.   Therefore, inventory management would not be a feature of a service.

144   B

The extent to which supply chain management is a strategic issue can be considered using Reck and Long's strategic positioning tool.

145   D

Total productive maintenance (TPM) engages all levels and functions of the organisation in maintenance. Workers are trained to take care of the equipment over its entire useful life.

146   D

Cousins' strategic supply wheel is made up of five spokes; organisation structure, relationships with suppliers, cost/benefit, competences and performance measures.

147   A, B and D

Regression analysis, expert opinion polls and the Delphi technique are all techniques used to forecast demand. Answers C and E (statistical process control and the 5-s practice) are techniques associated with quality management.

148   C

Liberalisation is another term for free trade. It would not be associated with operations management.

149 D

Computer numerical control (CNC) converts the design produced by computer aided design (CAD) into numbers. The numbers can be considered to be the co-ordinates of a graph and they control the exact movements of the machine allowing the creation of almost any desired pattern or shape.

150 B and C

The main features of a flexible manufacturing system (FMS) are the ability to change quickly from one job to another (answer B), fast response times (answer C) and small batch production (so answer A is incorrect). Answer D relates to a potential disadvantage of a FMS in that production line economies of scale may no longer be enjoyed.

151 C

A 'fixed position' and 'cellular manufacturing' are two approaches to layout.

152 D

Lobbyists seek to put their case to the government to influence legislative or regulative processes. Therefore, it would not be associated with quality improvement.

153 D

The 5S practice is an approach to achieving an organised, clean and standardised workplace and is often part of a Kaizen approach.

154 A

The four main supplier sourcing strategies available to firms are single, multiple, delegated and parallel.

155 A – TRUE

Taylor believed that by organising work in a scientific manner, the organisation's productivity will increase and this will enable the organisation to reward employees with the remuneration they desire (their main motivation).

156 D

The four quality-related costs are prevention, appraisal, internal failure and external failure.

157 A

EOQ stands for Economic Order Quantity. The model can be used to establish the optimum re-order quantity.

158 C

Both 5S and Six Sigma are frameworks for trying to improve work practices, particularly with respect to quality.

159 A

Lean management is a philosophy that aims to systematically eliminate waste.

160 A

A quality circle is a small group of employees, with a range of skills from all levels of the organisation. They meet voluntarily on a regular basis to discuss quality issues and to develop solutions to real problems.

161 A

The value system looks at linking the value chains of suppliers and customers to that of the organisation.

162 B

180 degree feedback may be used as part of the appraisal process. It collects anonymous or named views of the appraisee from their colleagues.

Five why examines quality issues by constantly asking 'why' until the real issue is identified. The 5-S practice in an approach to achieving an organised, clean and standardised workplace. Six sigma aims to reduce the number of faults that go beyond an accepted tolerance limit.

163 D

Juran drew on the Pareto principle and stated that 85% of quality problems are due to the systems that employees work within rather than the employees themselves. Answer A (an organised, clean and standardised workplace is the key to quality management) refers to the 5-S practice, answer B (managers should set up and then continually improve the systems in which people work) refers to Deming and Answer C (prevention of quality problems is key) refers to Crosby.

164 C

Total productive maintenance (TPM) engages all levels and functions of the organisation in maintenance. Workers are trained to take care of equipment.

165 A

The ABC system divides a company's inventory into different classifications – A, B or C. Managers can focus on items that account for the majority of their inventory. Category A items are of high value and usage whereas category C items are the least used and require little management control.

166 D

Japanese companies found the definition of quality as 'the degree of conformance to a standard' too narrow and consequently started to use a new definition of quality as 'user satisfaction'.

167 C

Continuous improvement in quality, productivity and effectiveness can be obtained by establishing management responsibility for processes as well as outputs.

168 B

It is now recognised that successful management of suppliers is based upon collaboration. A company should be able to improve quality and reduce costs as a result of this collaboration.

169 C

Computer aided design (CAD) and computer aided manufacturing (CAM) have resulted in innovative solutions to product design and can lead to the use of robots and computerised inventory management.

170 A and B

There are a number of Kaizen tools including the plan-do-check-act cycle, the fishbone diagram, the Pareto rule and the five why process. Answers C and D (cellular manufacturing and total productive maintenance) tend to be techniques associated with lean management.

171 A

Hammer defined BPR as a fundamental rethinking and radical redesign of business processes. This involves the themes listed.

172 D

A Materials Requirements Planning or MRP system creates a production schedule for end-products from existing and forecast customer demand quantities. It then uses the master production schedule, a bill of materials file, the inventory file and data about production times to produce a detailed schedule for the in-house manufacture of parts and sub-assemblies. It can also produce a purchase requirements schedule for raw materials and components.

An MRP system is not linked to the computer systems of other functions in the organisation, as described in answer A. MRP schedules production to meet actual and anticipated demand (so answer B is not correct), and is an alternative to scheduling production in economic batch quantities (so answer C is not correct).

173 C

A principle of TQM is that commitment to total quality calls for a TQM culture within the organisation, and all employees should be committed to quality improvement (answer C). The ideal level of defects is zero and there should not be any minimum acceptable level of defects (answer B is incorrect). Statistical quality control is used to monitor defects and provide control reports to management: TQM relies both on employee commitment and statistical quality control – so answer A is not correct. The aim should be to eliminate failure costs, such as costs arising from handling customer complaints, warranties and guarantees, damage to reputation and re-working rejected items. However, some costs relating to quality – prevention costs in particular – have to be incurred, so answer D is incorrect.

174   A

The different types of waste include:

- inventory
- waiting
- defective units
- effort
- transportation
- over-processing
- over-production.

175   C

Lean manufacturing is closely associated with JIT production. In lean manufacturing, production is initiated by customer demand (demand-pull) and products are made to order. Production should either be a continuous work flow, if there is continuous demand, or in small batch sizes. The ideal batch size is 1 – the customer's order. Large batches are not produced, because these create unwanted inventory.

There should be small work cells, with all the equipment needed to make the product and all the necessary labour skills: work cells in a small area that do all the work on a product eliminate waste from motion, transportation and waiting. Workers need to be multi-skilled, so that they can switch from one task to another as the situation requires.

176   D

Work flow design, with work organised in small work cells within a small area of the factory floor, can speed up production times and prevent inventory building up. Work flow can be arranged so as to reduce the physical movement of materials and people.

Production should be scheduled to meet customer demand; if necessary, there will be unused capacity. It is better to have several small machines than one large complex machine, because production will be more flexible. The aim should be to reduce set-up times between batches or jobs, because waiting is wasteful.

177   A

BPR seeks radical/transformational change in process (and the processes should be 're-engineered'). In contrast, 5S, 6 Sigma and quality circles are all based on the concept of continuous and incremental improvements.

178   B – FALSE

Reverse logistics is the return of unwanted or surplus goods, materials or equipment back to the organisation for reuse, recycling or disposal. The definition in the question refers to reverse engineering (not in the syllabus).

179 A – TRUE

Internet selling has increased the average level of returns received by an organisation and has resulted in an increased focus on their reverse logistics capability in order to reduce costs, improve customer service and increase revenue.

180 A

The need for correction shows that a failure has occurred, so the answer is A or B. If the corrective work is because a customer has sent the goods back, then it would be an external failure cost. The fact that there is scrap and materials have been lost would indicate that the problem was picked up before goods left the factory, making them internal failure costs.

181 D

Service – activities that ensure that customers enjoy their purchases by providing information systems, installation, training, maintenance, repair and breakdown assistance, etc.

182 B

You could argue that all four answers could be involved in why a firm decides to consider its supply chain in more detail. However, only answer B gives a direct cause of supply chain partnerships being established.

SYLLABUS SECTION E: MARKETING

183 C

Make sure you are familiar with current marketing techniques and the jargon that accompanies them.

184 D

Frequency of purchase is not a demographic factor.

185 B

Lancaster and Withey concluded that customers go through a five stage decision making process in any purchase:

1   Need recognition

2   Information search

3   Evaluation of alternatives

4   Decision to purchase

5   Post-purchase evaluation.

186 D

Secondary research is data that is already available (therefore, the use of a search engine would be an example of this). It is cheaper and quicker than primary research.

187 B

By definition.

188 A

By definition.

189 D

By definition.

190 D

Pricing includes elements such as basic price levels, discounts, payment terms and credit policy. It would not include commission for a sales team.

191 A

Market research will be required to understand the organisation's activities and to provide a basis for effective marketing decisions to be made. It should precede market segmentation.

192 C

Physical evidence is required to make the intangible service more tangible, e.g. previous customer testimonials or reviews.

193 A

Durable goods are relatively expensive and will not be purchased on a regular basis. Handmade shoes would be an example of a durable good. The other answers are examples of fast moving consumer goods.

194 A

By definition.

195 C

The recognised alternatives to a marketing orientation are a sales orientation, a production orientation and a product orientation.

196 C

This is a tough question as you could argue that D is also a correct answer. However, strictly speaking, market penetration should give you a larger share of an *existing* market, rather than access to a *larger* market, so C is the best answer.

197 D

The extended marketing mix consists of people, processes and physical evidence. Positioning involves the formulation of a definitive marketing strategy around which the product would be marketed to the target audience.

198 B

Direct marketing involves direct communication with the target customer, e.g. using direct mail or telemarketing.

199 B

Merit goods are considered so important that governments will choose to provide them rather than relying on market forces, thus ensuring that the poor do not miss out. Examples include education and healthcare.

200 B

Cognitive paradigm theory is based on the idea that a purchase is an outcome of problem solving. The consumer receives and makes sense of considerable quantities of information before choosing between products.

201 B

A production orientated manufacturer will focus on making as many units as possible in order to take advantage of economies of scale and hence reduce unit costs. A major task of management is to pursue improved production and distribution efficiency. Answer A, product orientated, refers to a manufacturer that centres its activities on continually refining and improving its products. Answers C and D are irrelevant.

202 A

Durable goods are a relatively expensive type of consumer good. They tend to be bought on an irregular basis, e.g. a new TV or car. The decision to purchase will be influenced by the age of the existing product, new technical features and changing fashion trends.

203

Term	Definition
Relationship marketing	The technique of maintaining and exploiting the firm's customer base as a means of developing new business opportunities.
Postmodern marketing	A philosophical approach to marketing which focuses on giving the customer an experience that is customised to them and in ensuring they receive marketing messages in a form they prefer.
Internal marketing	A means of applying the philosophy and practices of marketing to the organisation's employees.
Product orientation	The business centres its activities on continually improving and refining its products, assuming that customers simply want the best quality for their money.

204   A – TRUE

Ansoff devised a matrix showing possible strategies for products or markets. It can assist in positioning the organisation's products.

205   D

'Pull' marketing is aimed at persuading end-consumers to demand a product from distributors (such as retailers), which in turn will result in the distributor wanting to stock and sell the item. TV advertising is an example of a promotion that could be intended to have this 'pull' effect.

206   A

An analysis of past sales (answer C) will provide information about total sales, but not about how many customers buy the product, nor in what quantities or how frequently. Observation is useful for looking at a customer's buying habits, but does not provide information about the numbers of customers for a product or the frequency of buying. Group interviews can be useful for obtaining information about customer attitudes/consumer attitudes, but the group size is fairly small and so cannot provide reliable estimates of sales measurements.

Sample surveys in different geographical areas are likely to provide reasonably reliable information about numbers of customers, buying quantities and buying frequency.

207   A and E

Services are heterogeneous (not homogenous) and do not result in the transfer of property.

208   B

Internal marketing is an activity aimed at getting employees who come into contact with customers (e.g. after-sales service staff, counter staff and floor staff in shops, customer service call centre staff) to recognise the need to meet customer requirements – and training them how to do this.

209   C

By definition.

210   C

The gatekeeper starts the process of collecting information on the purchase. Deciders make the final decision regarding which product to buy. Approvers will approve and therefore authorise the final decision. Sellers, on the other hand, do not form a part of the decision making process for purchasing a product or service.

211   B

Public relations is part of the promotional mix. It involves the creation of positive attitudes regarding products, services or companies by various means, including unpaid media coverage and involvement with community activities.

212 A

Market penetration involves charging a low price initially in order to gain rapid growth in market share.

213 C

Skim pricing involves the setting of a high price for a new product in order to benefit from those wishing to be early adopters of the product.

214 D

Undifferentiated marketing is the delivery of a single product to the market with little concern for segment analysis.

215 C

Direct marketing, branding activities and public relations campaigns are all examples of promotion.

216 A

Loss leader pricing refers to the sale of certain products at a loss in order to generate customer loyalty or more sales of other products.

217 C

The product life cycle shows sales volume against time.

218 C

A product orientated organisation concentrates its product features on those it instinctively believes to be right.

219 B – FALSE

Cash cows are characterised by low market growth and high market share where as a question mark will be in a high growth market but will have low market share.

220 B, C, D and E

Features of B2B marketing include derived demand, fewer buyers, high purchasing power, close relationships between buyers and sellers and technical complexity.

SYLLABUS SECTION F: MANAGING HUMAN RESOURCES

221 B

By definition.

222 A

Psychological contracts exist between individuals and the organisations to which they belong.

223 A

Remember that 'recruitment' involves attracting suitable candidates but it is the 'selection' stage where we choose the best people from the field of candidates. This is where assessment centres would be used.

224 B

An assessment centre brings together a group of applicants for a job or a number of jobs (for example, graduate trainee management positions) and the applicants are put through a variety of intensive assessments in a period of one to three days.

225 A

Psychological contracts exist between individuals and the organisations to which they belong, be they work or social, and normally take the form of implied and unstated expectations. According to Handy, individuals have sets of results that they expect from organisations – results that will satisfy their needs and in return for which they will expend some of their energies and talents. Similarly, organisations have sets of expectations of individuals and a list of payments and outcomes that they will give to the individuals.

226 B – FALSE

It is true that personnel motivates staff by payment and coercion and that human resource management motivates staff by consent and involvement. However, personnel views employees as costs whereas human resource management views employees as assets.

227 A, D and F

The other three components of Guest's model are HRM practices, a set of HRM outcomes and a number of performance outcomes.

228 A – True

Stage 4 may involve the creation and use of a number of plans such as a recruitment plan and a training plan.

229 D

Cattell's 16PF test is a selection test. It provides 16 basic dimensions, e.g. extrovert/ introvert, along with scores from 0 – 10.

230

Stage	Description
Selection	Choosing the best person for the job from a field of candidates sourced via recruitment.
Appraisal	Systematic review and assessment of an employee's performance, potential and training needs.
Training	Formal learning to achieve the level of skills, knowledge and competence to carry out the current role.
Development	Realisation of a person's potential through formal and informal learning to enable them to carry out their current and future role.

231 C

Recruitment involves attracting suitable candidates and so could include advertising.

232 B

Remember that 'recruitment' involves attracting suitable candidates but it is the 'selection' stage where we choose the best people from the field of candidates. This is where assessment centres and psychometric testing would be used.

233 A

The CIMA code of ethics is an example of a principles-based approach as opposed to a rules-based approach.

234 B

Kolb is best known for his experiential learning cycle model.

235 D

In a panel interview a number of people interview the candidate simultaneously.

236 A and D

Psychometric and aptitude testing may be used as part of the selection process. Answer B (sequential) is an interview method whereas answers C and E (contrived and realistic) are types of system testing.

237 D

Handy's concept states that each of the three leaves of the shamrock is symbolic of a different group of people within the organisation: the professional core of employees; the contractual fringe where all work that could be done by someone else is contracted out; and the flexible labour force includes all those part-time workers and temporary workers.

238 B

Job analysis and selection occur before the person becomes an employee. Only a rather cynical organisation would aim to manipulate a new employee.

239 C

Interviewing is part of selection rather than recruitment, and contract negotiation follow these.

240 D

A key word in the question is 'effective'. Effective appraisal requires a dialogue between the manager and the person being appraised (the 'appraisee'). Any problems with the appraisee's work or performance are identified and should be discussed and resolved constructively. Answer C, in contrast, describes an ineffective appraisal process.

241 B – FALSE

A competency framework should regularly be updated by the employer (not the employee) to assess whether the employee still has the appropriate skills and abilities needed for the role.

242 B

The correct answer can probably be worked out by common sense. A test cannot be contradictory, although the results from tests can be, so answer A cannot be correct. The fact that tests are general in nature does not means that test results will vary over time, so answer C is not correct.

This leaves a choice between the tests being unreliable or unstable. If test results vary over time, this means that the tests are unreliable, but there is no reason to suppose that they might be unstable.

243 C

Succession planning involves 'grooming' an individual to take over in a key position after the present job-holder retires or moves on. This should ensure that the person who will take over has been given the necessary training and development programme to take over and do the work competently (answer C). A new person in a key job will not necessarily continue to do things in the same way as his predecessor; therefore answer B is incorrect. Succession planning is connected to promotion policy, where successors are appointed internally: however, the purpose of succession planning should not be to create promotion opportunities and answer A is not correct.

244 B

Recruitment is the process of attracting individuals into applying for a job. Employment agencies do this, usually by advertising or notifying the vacancy to individuals on their books. Screening is the process of vetting applications and removing those that are inappropriate and unlikely to be successful. The remaining applications are then passed to the company, whose responsibility it should be to select candidates for interview and make the selection.

245 A

If the employee's claim is correct, the employer would be liable for constructive dismissal, which is a form of unfair dismissal. A contract with a sub-contractor is subject to contract law, not employment law: the sub-contractor could claim breach of contract. It is probably considered reasonable to dismiss an employee who can no longer perform his job, such as a lorry driver who cannot drive (in the UK, on the assumption that there is no other job that the individual can do). Dismissal on the grounds of redundancy is also legal, although the employer must comply with redundancy procedures and legislation.

246 A

Job evaluation is used to assess what the value of a job is to the organisation, and so what an appropriate level of basic pay ought to be. With knowledge work, it is often difficult to carry out a reliable, objective job evaluation.

Benchmarking can be used to establish a pay level by looking at basic pay in similar jobs in other organisations (so answer B is not correct). If there is a scarcity of knowledge skills, this will put upward pressure on basic pay levels, but does not create a serious problem for setting pay levels (so answer C is not correct). Performance evaluation is an issue with performance-related pay, but not basic pay (so answer D is not correct).

247 D

Feedback being poorly delivered is an example of confrontation. The manager viewing appraisal as purely a form filling exercise is an example of bureaucracy.

248 D

References from a former employer are notoriously unreliable as a guide to future performance, or the candidate's character and abilities. The former employer is usually unwilling to criticise the individual, and concerned about any liability that might arise. However, a reference (on headed notepaper) should confirm that the candidate did actually work in the job, as stated in his/her job application, and that the employee was not dismissed for bad conduct.

249 D

Job evaluation is primarily a process by which the value of a job is assessed and a suitable rate of pay is decided accordingly. If different jobs are evaluated with the same scoring system, the rates of pay for the different jobs can be set in relation to each other, according to their respective total scores in the evaluation exercise.

250 D

Answers A and B refer to profit-related pay and answer C describes either piece work payment or payment by the hour/day.

251 B

The process of recruitment is the attraction of a field of suitable candidates. Selection is choosing one from that number.

252

Learning style	Explanation
Theorist	Adapt and integrate information in a step-by-step logical way.
Reflector	Prefer to step back to ponder and observe others before taking action.
Pragmatist	Are keen to try out new ideas, theories and techniques to see if they work in practise.
Activist	Involve themselves fully and without bias in new experiences.

253 A

Recruitment agencies are commonly used by organisations, and much training is carried out by external training specialists. For the relocation of staff from one geographical location to another, external specialists are also used. It is much more difficult to outsource staff development, where a detailed knowledge of individuals and their progress and experience within the organisation is required.

254 D

Part A section 5.3 of Ethical Guidelines if you're really keen, or common sense otherwise. None of the other options are reasonable.

255 B

The levels from 1 to 4 are Reaction, learning, behaviour, results.

256 D

Equal opportunities is concerned with giving fair and non-discriminatory treatment to all job applicants and existing employees. Its purpose is to remove discrimination and it relies on proactive action to achieve this. It is a Human Resources role to promote and ensure equal opportunities within the organisation.

Diversity is about maximising the potential of all individuals within the organisation. It is relevant to all employees, not only those in disadvantaged groups. It is a managerial role.

257 D

There are limited grounds for redundancy. Redundancy can occur where a role is no longer required. Roles become redundant and this is not linked to individual conduct or performance. Where there is cessation of a business or part of a business or of certain activities within a business then redundancy can be justified. Which of the following is NOT a requirement of effective delegation?

The fab five on a European night that shook the world

Number 5 in '05. A fresh chapter in our proud history. Destiny came calling and now a new generation can take their place alongside the famous heroes of the past. Relive the magic of Istanbul and enjoy again the greatest footballing story ever told. Walk on . . .

Trinity Mirror Sport Media

Printed by Pensord www.pensord.co.uk

EXECUTIVE EDITOR Ken Rogers • EDITOR Steve Hanrahan • PRODUCTION EDITOR Paul Dove • ART EDITOR Rick Cooke
DESIGN TEAM Barry Parker, Colin Sumpter, Glen Hind, Lee Ashun WRITERS Chris McLoughlin, Gavin Kirk, Alan Jewell, David Randles
MARKETING EXECUTIVE Dave Rad • PRINTERS Pensord • PHOTOGRAPHIC AGENCIES Main partners: Empics, Trinity Mirror
LFC TICKET OFFICE 24 HOUR INFO LINE 0870 444 4949 • LFC CREDIT CARD LINE (TICKETS) 0870 220 2151
MAGAZINE SALES MANAGER Elizabeth Morgan 0151 285 8412 • ADVERTISING 0151 285 8412
SUBSCRIPTIONS 0845 1430001 (International +44 845 1430001) • Subscriptions online www.liverpoolfc.tv/match/magazine
email lfcmagazine@sportmedia-tm.com • Write to: LFC Magazine, Sport Media PO BOX 48 Old Hall Street, Liverpool L69 3EB

Red sky at night,
Turkish delight

It's ours to Keep

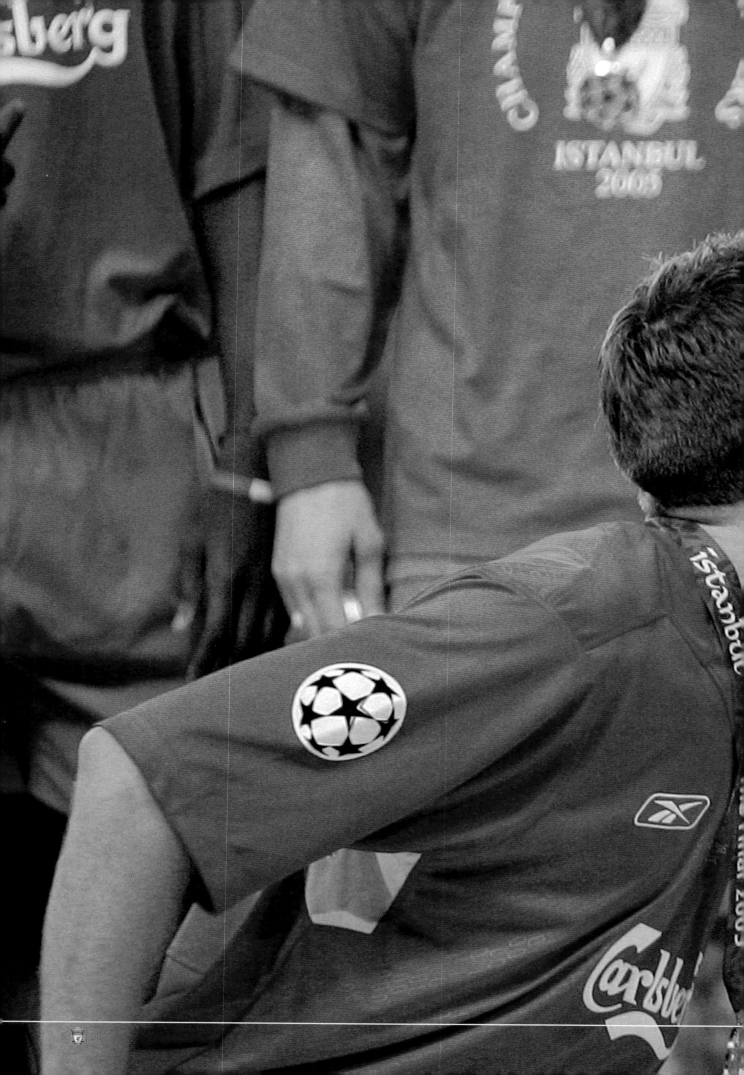

It's ours to Keep

From the agony...

...to the ecstasy

The Joy of Six

Probably the best six minutes you'll ever have!
3-0 down, with seemingly no way back.
But this is Liverpool we're talking about...

54 mins: Stevie G starts the comeback with a leap of faith

56 mins: Vladimir Smicer makes it two with a ferocious shot

59 mins: A typical Gerrard burst through
the Milan defence forces a penalty

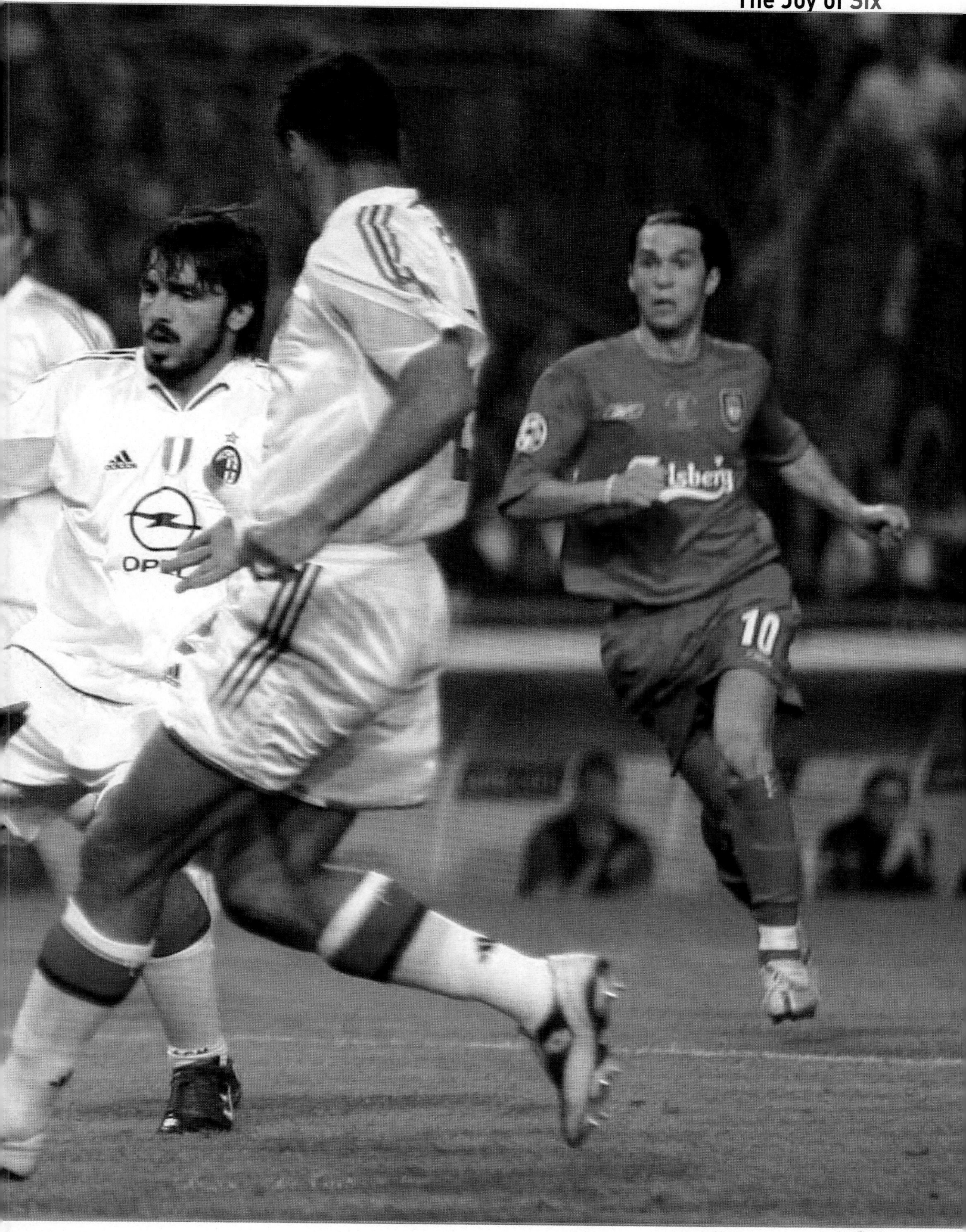
adidas
OPEL
10

60 mins: Second time lucky as Alonso follows up the penalty rebound

On the spot again for European glory

From Rome '84 to Istanbul '05. Wobbly legs all round. We kept our nerve and the Cup was ours with a little help from Jerzy and our shoot-out heroes. If you're still hiding behind the settee, it's safe to come out now . . .

Number one Jerzy: AC Milan's Serginho blazes the first penalty over the bar (far left); Dudek saves from Andrea Pirlo (centre) and it's all too much for Kaka and his team-mates during the shoot-out

How the drama unfolded from the spot . . .

0-0 AC Milan substitute Serginho slices his shot high and wide after Jerzy Dudek had danced on the line.

1-0 Dietmar Hamann shimmies on his run-up before confidently despatching his spot-kick to Dida's right

1-0 Italian international Andrea Pirlo makes it two blanks for AC Milan as Dudek dives to his right to save

2-0 Liverpool substitute Djibril Cisse calmly sidefoots the ball home, sending the keeper the wrong way

2-1 Former Newcastle striker Jon Dahl Tomasson isn't put off by Dudek and blasts his spot-kick in to the corner

2-1 John Arne Riise places his kick low to the keeper's right but Dida stretches to save

2-2 Not even Dudek's Bruce Grobbelaar-style wobbly legs can put off Kaka as the Brazil midfielder sends the Liverpool keeper the wrong way

3-2 Vladimir Smicer keeps his nerve to sidefoot into the net

3-2 Liverpool win after Andriy Shevchenko's penalty is saved

Didi beats Dida: Dietmar Hamann finds the corner of the net beating the AC Milan keeper to make it 1-0 in the shoot-out

A tale of two keepers . . .

There's no hiding place if you're a goalkeeper in a Champions League final penalty shoot-out. While Jerzy Dudek (left) salutes the fans after Milan had missed their first penalty, it's agony for Dida who looks to the heavens after failing to keep out Vladimir Smicer's spot-kick as the Reds marched on to glory

Take five: The moment
history is made as
Jerzy Dudek saves from
Andriy Shevchenko to
give Liverpool a 3-2
shoot-out victory

On your marks: The faces say it all and the celebrations can begin

We couldn't have done it without you...

Them Scousers again...

The Travelling Kop in Istanbul

The North Shield
Pub & Restaurant

FOR THOSE OF YOU WATCHING
IN BLUE AND WHITE, THIS IS
WHAT A EUROPEAN
CUP LOOKS LIKE....

SUPERCROATIGORBISCAN
USED TO BEATROCIOUS

HE PUT NEDVED TO BED
AND KEPT EIDUR DOWN
NOW SHEVCHENKO CAN'T SLEEP
COS CARRA'S IN TOWN

Painting the town Red

Back home in Liverpool...

THE ALBERT
A Place to Meet · A Hearty Welcome

Game on...

LIVERPOOL FC

SOME SAY IM
A DREAMER
BUT IM NOT THE
ONLY ONE

Game over...?

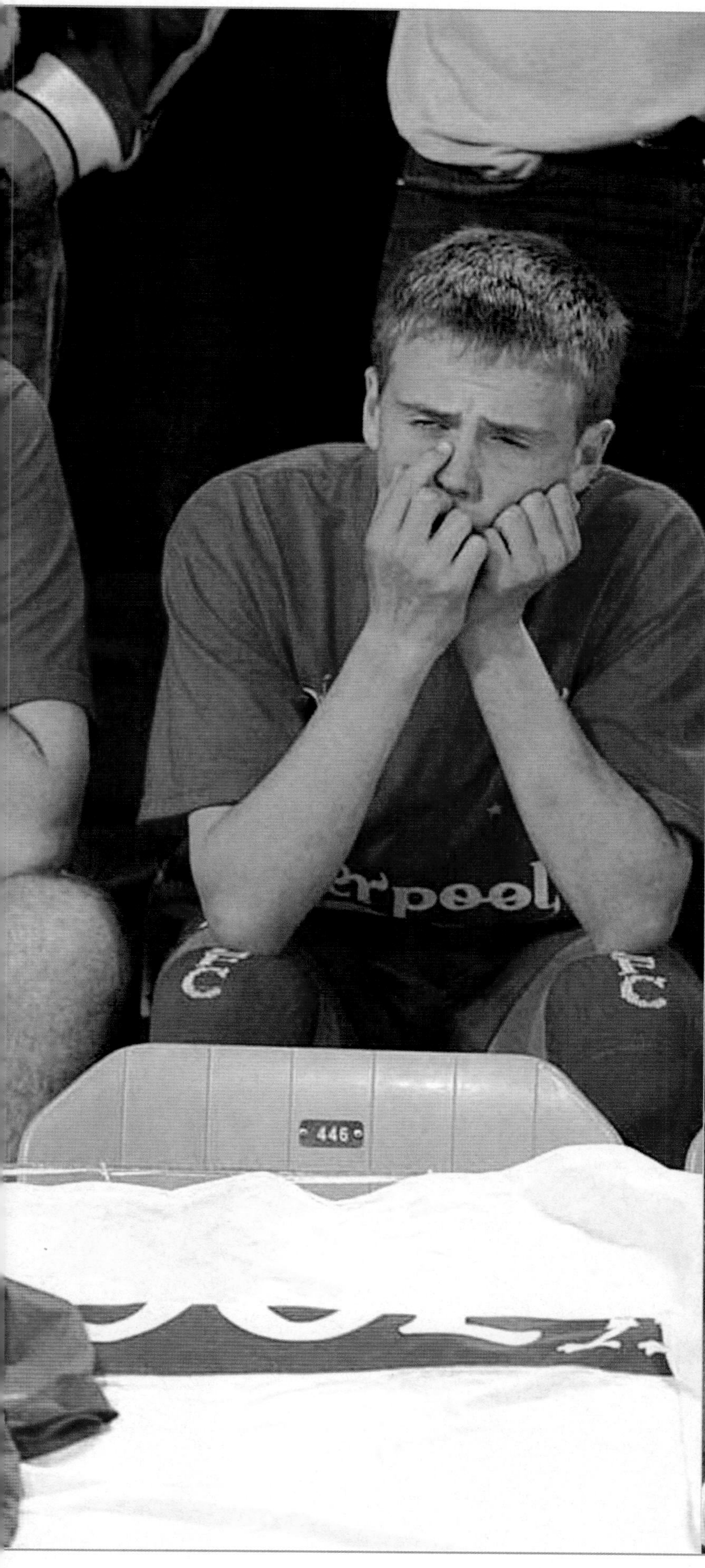
446

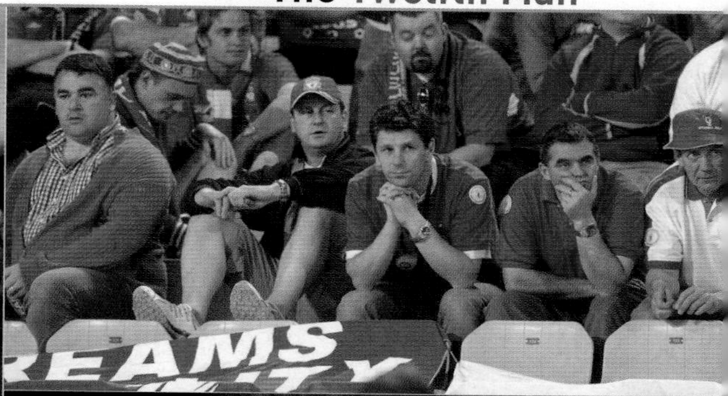
REAMS

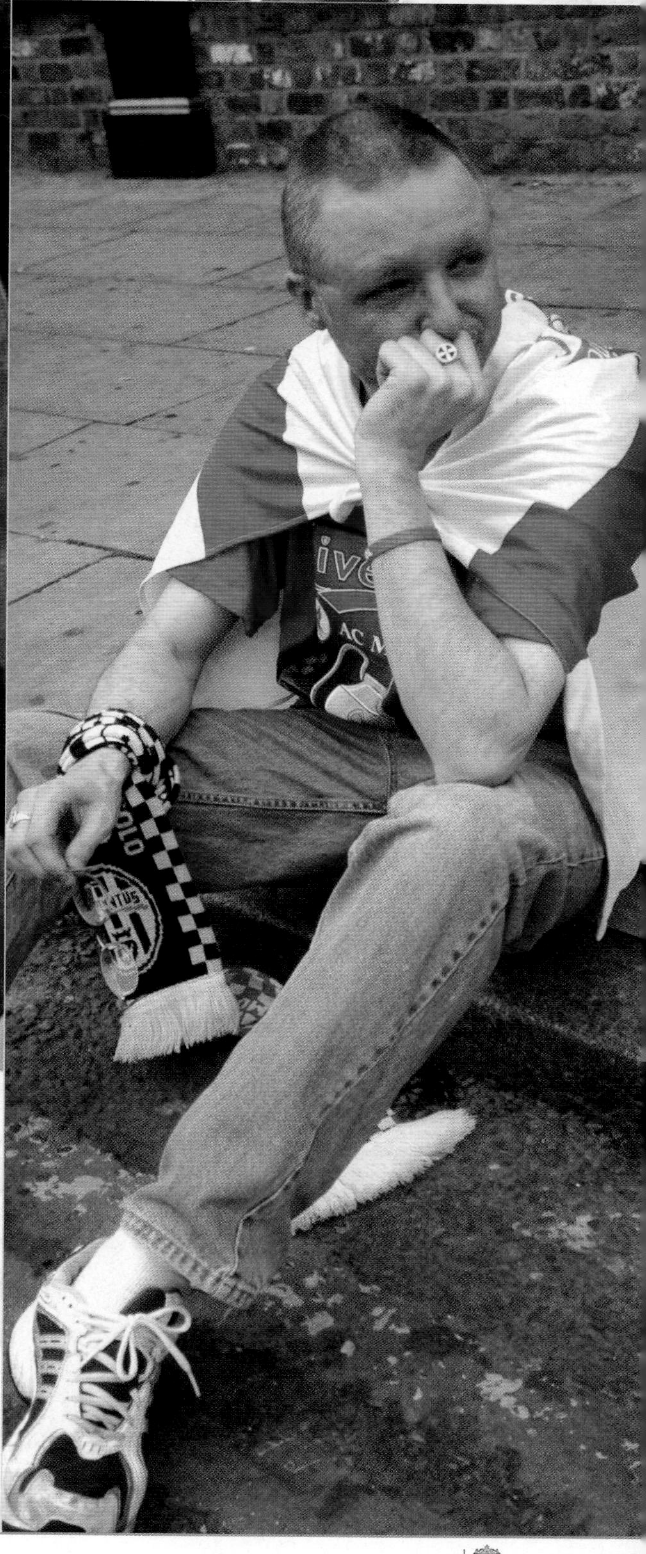

Game of a lifetime...

Gateway
to heaven

Hangin' out on the Paisley gates.
Maybe one day they'll be
making them for Rafa

History

1977, 1978, 1981, 1984 . . . 2005. It's ours to keep. The
memories of what happened on May 25 in the Ataturk
Stadium, Istanbul, can never be taken away from us . . .

Makers

Chapter Five

Above: The early goal from Paolo Maldini was a total shock
Below: Let's start again boys . . .

You're the Bos-phor-us:
Stevie G shares his
emotions with Rafa

My ball: You won't pass the
pass master, Xabi Alonso

History Makers

Above: Djimi Traore concedes
an early free-kick leading to
Milan's shock opening goal

Right: Milan versus Milan.
The livewire Baros keeps
Jaap Stam busy

istanbul
The Final 2005
istanbul
2005
istanbul
CHAMPIONS LEAGUE
ISTANBUL
2005
The Final 2005

Team Liverpool:
Spirit is high in the
Reds camp

Left: Shooting for glory.
Luis Garcia lets fly

Right: Heads we win.
Milan Baros climbs
highest to beat Paolo
Maldini to the ball

Below: Riise tries to get
to grips with Kaka

Fresh legs: Djibril Cisse
causes Gattuso problems

Destiny: The moment they said our name was on the cup. Jerzy Dudek makes a brilliant double save from Andriy Shevchenko late in extra time

'Defying the odds has been the script of Liverpool's Champions League campaign, yet the story of how Steven Gerrard came to get his hands on the club's fairytale fifth continental crown defies belief'

– The Daily Post

'Yes, yes, yes, Liverpool have at last got the fresh chapter for their gilded story book for which they ached so long'

– The Daily Express

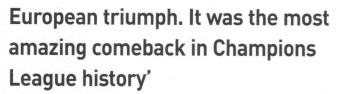

'This was certainly Liverpool's greatest ever European triumph. It was the most amazing comeback in Champions League history'

– The Daily Star

'The glory of Liverpool is reborn. They are not merely the champions of Europe once more but the creators of a victory that will be talked about so long as football exists'

– The Guardian

'They never walk alone along Anfield Road. But the magnificent men in red, who emerged from this extraordinary match with the European Cup, now walk in the company of legends'

— The Daily Mail

'It is a day for sharing the unbridled joy of younger fans who've heard all too much about the feats from Liverpool's past but who now have one of their own to rank alongside, if not above, all the others'

— The Liverpool Echo

'They are a new breed of Anfield heroes who somehow, from somewhere, found the courage to conjure the greatest comeback there has ever been' – The Daily Mirror

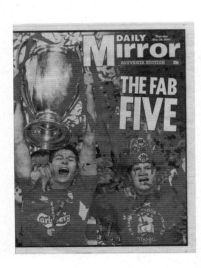

It's
back
for
good

Homecoming

Best of the
action along
the way...

From the Arnold Schwarzenegger stadium in Austria to the Ataturk.
It's been an epic crusade. Rafa's red and white army returned from
the principality of kings and the land of the gods with battle scars.
But a fortress was built on the fields of Anfield Road. Our troops regrouped,
we crossed the Rhine, scaled the Italian Alps and the Bridge was finally taken.
These are just some of the enduring images from an historic conquest...

All systems Monaco: Djibril Cisse opens the scoring at Anfield

Deft finish: Milan Baros makes it 2-0 against Monaco at Anfield and the players are quick to celebrate (top left)

Centre left: Luis Garcia tries to make an impact in the 1-0 defeat at Olympiakos, but it's the Greek fans who enjoyed the night

No way through: Cisse and the boys draw
a blank at home to Deportivo La Coruna

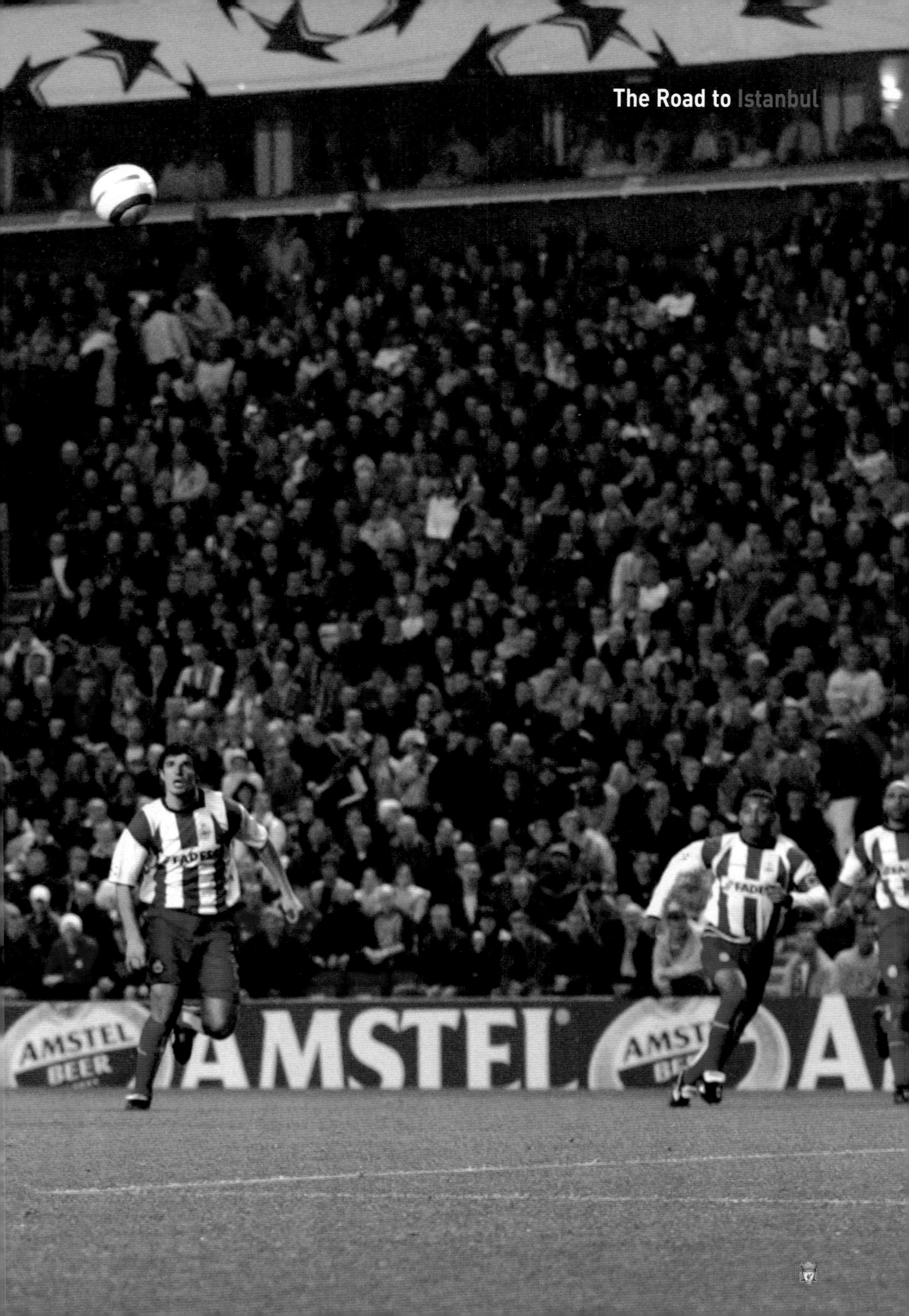
AMSTEL
BEER
AMSTEL
AMSTEL
BEER

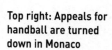

Top right: Appeals for handball are turned down in Monaco

Top left: Under pressure from Baros, Deportivo's Jorge Andrade puts John Arne Riise's cross into his own net in Spain

Bottom: Flo, Mellor, and Stevie G celebrate the remarkable comeback against Olympiakos at Anfield

Kop that: Anfield goes wild as Stevie celebrates his stunning winner against Olympiakos

Sittin' on the dock of the Bay: Luis Garcia is the hero again as the Reds destroy Leverkusen home and away

Ju beauty: Garcia scores one of the goals of
the tournament to stun Juventus at Anfield

Juve done us proud: The Liverpool players salute the fans after a stirling performance in Italy

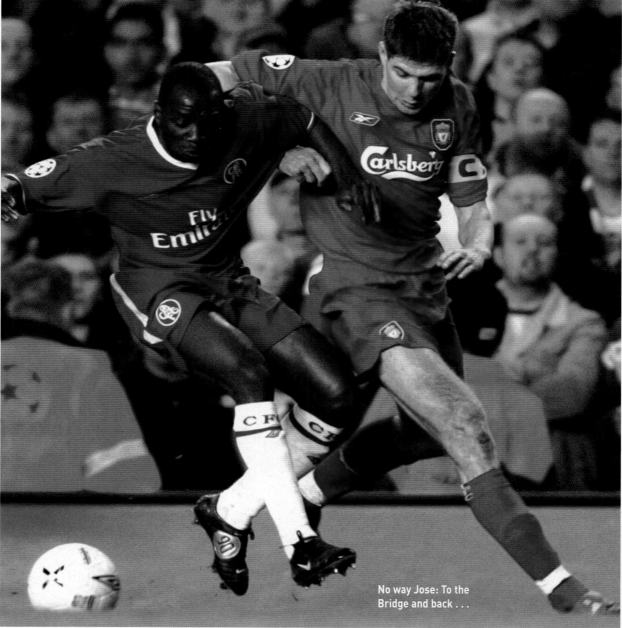

No way Jose: To the
Bridge and back . . .

Tell me ma, me ma, the cabinet is not
quite full, we're going to Istanbul...

The glory that was Rome

25 May 1977

LIVERPOOL 3
McDermott 28, Smith 64,
Neal (pen) 82

BORUSSIA MOENCHENGLADBACH 1
Simonsen 52

We three kings: Ray Kennedy,
Terry McDermott and Jimmy Case
parade the European Cup

Right:
Tommy Smith celebrates a famous goal

Paisley's red and white army in full force

Sealed with a kiss: The sweet taste of
success for Phil Neal and Jimmy Case

Hat's my boy: Skipper Emlyn Hughes
takes his hat off to the Liverpool fans

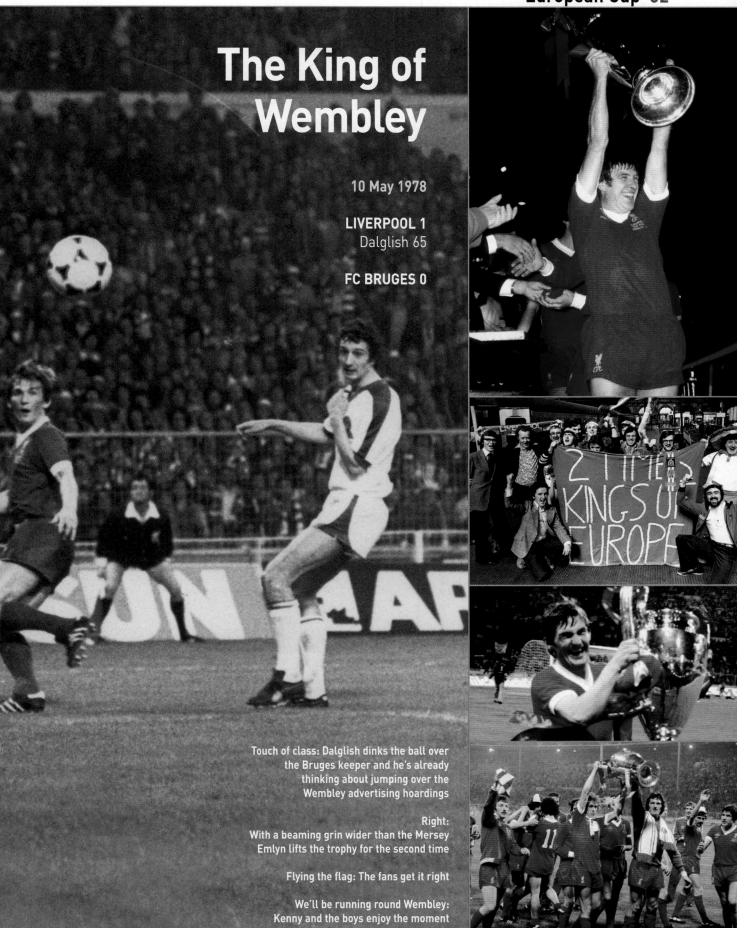

The King of Wembley

10 May 1978

LIVERPOOL 1
Dalglish 65

FC BRUGES 0

Touch of class: Dalglish dinks the ball over
the Bruges keeper and he's already
thinking about jumping over the
Wembley advertising hoardings

Right:
With a beaming grin wider than the Mersey
Emlyn lifts the trophy for the second time

Flying the flag: The fans get it right

We'll be running round Wembley:
Kenny and the boys enjoy the moment

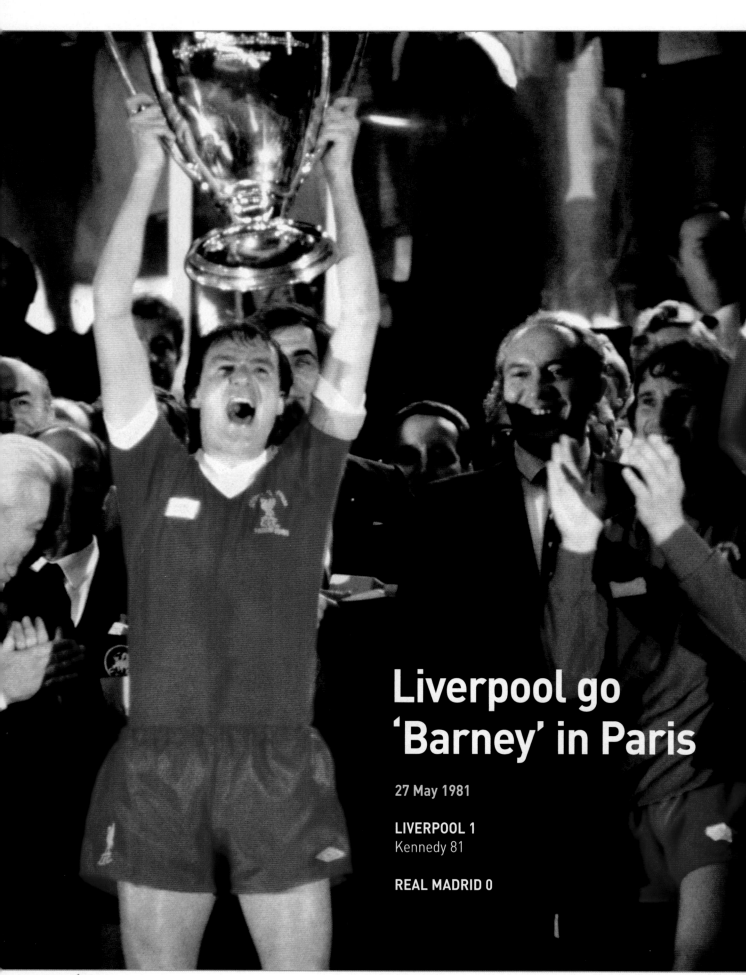

Liverpool go 'Barney' in Paris

27 May 1981

LIVERPOOL 1
Kennedy 81

REAL MADRID 0

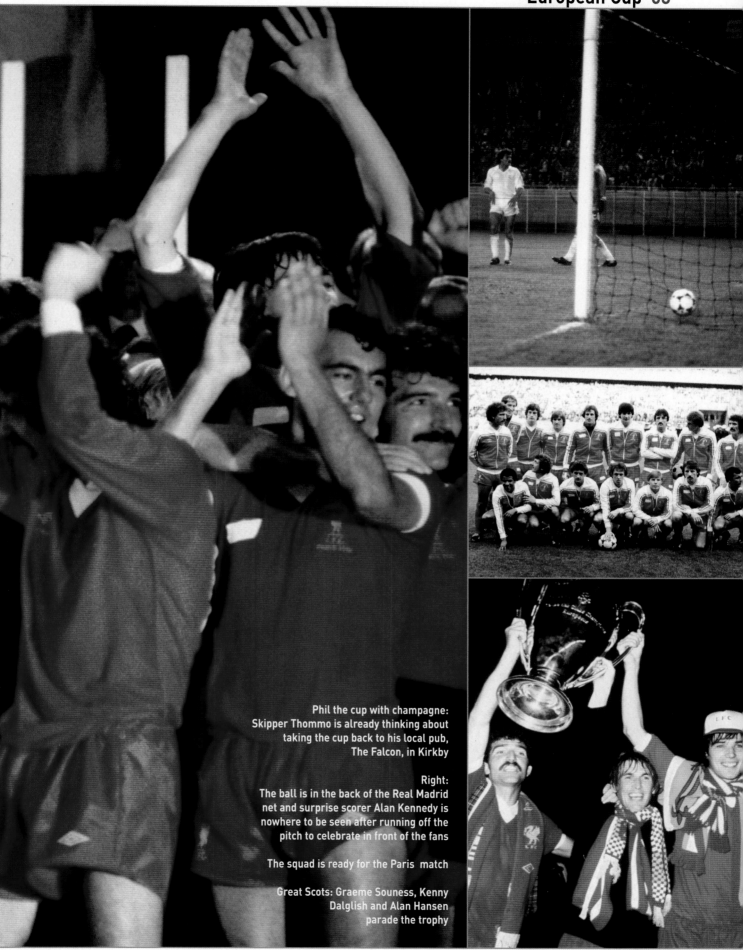

Phil the cup with champagne:
Skipper Thommo is already thinking about
taking the cup back to his local pub,
The Falcon, in Kirkby

Right:
The ball is in the back of the Real Madrid
net and surprise scorer Alan Kennedy is
nowhere to be seen after running off the
pitch to celebrate in front of the fans

The squad is ready for the Paris match

Great Scots: Graeme Souness, Kenny
Dalglish and Alan Hansen
parade the trophy

Beaten in their own back yard

30 May 1984

LIVERPOOL 1
Neal 15

ROMA 1
Pruzzo 43

Liverpool won 4-2 on
penalties after extra-time
(scorers: Neal, Souness,
Rush, A. Kennedy)

What a start: Phil Neal sneaks up
for the opening goal

Right:
Four-midable: The Reds celebrate again

Wobbly legs: Brucie puts Graziani off in the
penalty shoot-out

Roman invasion: This time it's Fagan's army

Cool, calm and the ball is collected
by Grobbelaar

IST-UNBULIEVABLE

25 May 2005

LIVERPOOL 3
Gerrard 54
Smicer 56
Alonso 60

AC MILAN 3
Maldini 1
Crespo 39
Crespo 44

Liverpool won 3-2 on penalties after extra-time (scorers: Hamann, Cisse Smicer)

ISBN 1905266049

9 781905 266043